Loving Our Enemies

Christ shaping Adam, Chartres Cathedral

Loving Our Enemies

REFLECTIONS ON
THE HARDEST COMMANDMENT

by

Jim Forest

ORBIS BOOKS
Maryknoll, New York

ORBIS BOOKS
Maryknoll, New York 10545

Fathers and Brothers
MARYKNOLL™

Founded in 1970, Orbis Books endeavors to publish works that enlighten the mind, nourish the spirit, and challenge the conscience. The publishing arm of the Maryknoll Fathers and Brothers, Orbis seeks to explore the global dimensions of the Christian faith and mission, to invite dialogue with diverse cultures and religious traditions, and to serve the cause of reconciliation and peace. The books published reflect the views of their authors and do not represent the official position of the Maryknoll Society. To learn more about Maryknoll and Orbis Books, please visit our website at www.maryknollsociety.org.

Library of Congress Cataloging-in-Publication Data

Forest, Jim (James H.)
    Loving our enemies : reflections on the hardest commandment / Jim Forest.
        pages cm
    Includes bibliographical references.
    ISBN 978-1-62698-090-7 (pbk.)
    1. Love—Religious aspects—Christianity. 2. Enemies—Religious aspects—Christianity. I. Title.
BV4639.F578 2014
241'.4—dc23
                                                                2014005483

To all of our grandchildren so far

Zackary
Kara
Noah
Joshua
Lux
Dylan
Sara
Julia

Far from being the pious injunction of a utopian dreamer,
this command [to love our enemies] is an absolute necessity
for the survival of our civilization.
Yes, it is love that will save our world and our civilization,
love even for enemies.

—Martin Luther King Jr.
Sermon at Dexter Avenue Baptist Church
November 17, 1957

To make peace with an enemy,
one must work with that enemy,
and that enemy becomes one's partner.

—Nelson Mandela
Long Walk to Freedom

If we believe in the Incarnation of the Son of God,
there should be no one on earth
in whom we are not prepared to see, in mystery,
the presence of Christ.

—Thomas Merton
New Seeds of Contemplation

Contents

Introduction

NOT EVERYTHING JESUS TAUGHT must be regarded as a commandment. Take, for example, his encounter with a wealthy young man who wanted to know what he needed to do in order to obtain eternal life. Referring to the ten basic laws given to Moses, Jesus told him not to murder, not to commit adultery, not to steal, not to give false testimony, to honor his father and mother, and to love his neighbor as himself. The young man replied that he had been following those rules throughout his life, but then asked a second question, "What do I still lack?" Jesus responded, "If you want to be perfect, go, sell your possessions and give to the poor, and you will have treasure in heaven. Then come, follow me" (Matthew 19:16-20). This was more than his questioner could bear. He went away sad, unable to embrace so radical an invitation.

It would be interesting to know what choices the young man made later in life. Perhaps he eventually became as poor as Saint Francis of Assisi. What is clear, however, is that the invitation Jesus gave him that day was not a commandment. It was what theologians sometimes have called a "counsel of perfection"—a teaching one may embrace but which is not a precondition for salvation for every Christian. In fact there are many saints included in the calendar of the church who had possessions and at least a few who were wealthy. Similarly, celibacy has always been a respected option for Christians—Jesus was unmarried—but it has always been seen as an option suitable only for a small minority of Christ's followers.

One cannot say that about love of enemies. It's not in the "if you would be perfect" category. It's basic Christianity. Jesus teaches it through direct instruction, through parables, and by the example given with his own life.

Love of enemies is not our default setting. It's a hard teaching,

1

as hard for me as it is for anyone. Our natural inclination is to hate those who have done us harm or seem prepared to do so.

But in my own case I had a head start in practicing this hardest of commandments. Growing up in America in the 1950s, it so happened that my parents were the enemy—not my personal enemy, but they were widely regarded as enemies. The reason was that they were Communists. The Cold War was at its iciest and McCarthyism at high tide. When I was celebrating my eleventh birthday, my father was in prison; it took nearly half a year for bail to be raised so that he might be free while awaiting trial. His arrest as a "top Red" had been coast-to-coast front-page news in 1952. Eventually, while my father's case was pending before the Supreme Court, the charges against him were dropped; but he, my mother, and others like them remained very much on America's enemy list throughout my childhood. The FBI not only kept close tabs on my parents but even fingerprinted my brother and me one afternoon when our mother was out of the house.

As a child I gradually became aware of my parent's dissident views, though I didn't understand them. That they were out of step with society as whole did not make them unlovable. Though my parents were divorced, they never spoke ill of each other, and both were loving parents. I wasn't even aware at the time how unusual it was for a white family (my mother, brother, and I) to be living in a mainly black neighborhood. I loved my parents, not for their political and philosophical beliefs, which I knew little about and was unable to understand, but for who they were.

If only we knew our enemies not just for what we think they believe but for who they are, Jesus' commandment to love them would be much easier. We might continue hating what our enemies stand for or the damage they may be causing, yet no longer hate them as persons or do anything to cause them harm.

If my mother especially provided an inspiring example, in early adulthood I was to come under the influence of another woman who gave an even more challenging witness to a life free of enmity: Dorothy Day. Following my discharge from the U.S. Navy, I became

Dorothy Day

part of the Catholic Worker community in New York City, led by Dorothy, and there discovered a person who not only refused to hate enemies but related to them in a way that could only be described as loving. Her life centered on hospitality. The writing of this small book draws deeply on what I learned—at least *began* to learn—in her company.

I am fortunate too that, thanks to Dorothy, I developed a deep relationship with the writer and Trappist monk Thomas Merton, another person who hated no one. In one of his letters to me he stressed the importance of seeing people, including adversaries, simply as fellow human beings. "One of the most important things to do is to keep cutting deliberately through political lines and barriers," he advised me in one letter, "and emphasizing that these are largely fabrications and that there is a genuine reality, totally opposed to the fictions of politics: the human dimension."

When I recall others I've had the privilege of knowing who exemplified love of enemies, I think of Russians I met in the 1980s when I was writing first one book and then a second about religious life in what was then the Soviet Union. Meeting and interviewing hundreds of Christians, often people who had close relatives who suffered and died in the archipelago of prison camps known as the Gulag, not once did I meet anyone who exhibited hatred or sought vengeance.

I will never forget a conversation one evening with a Russian Orthodox priest, Father Mikhail, in the ancient walled town of Novgorod. It was 1987. Mikhail Gorbachev, now in his second year as Soviet head of state, had brought religious persecution to a halt. I asked Father Mikhail, "Aren't you surprised?" "Not at all," he replied. "All believers have been praying for this every day of our lives. We knew God would answer our prayer, only we did not know when. I am only surprised that our prayer has been answered while I am still alive." "Still," I said, "surely you must hate those who caused so much suffering and who killed so many." "Christ does not hate them," Father Mikhail answered. "Why should I? How will they find the way to belief unless we love them? And if I refuse to love them, I too am not a believer."

My hope for this book is that it will play a part in making the love of enemies a goal worth striving toward in the daily lives of its readers, however much an uphill climb it may be. As Dorothy Day wrote in a journal entry, "The burdens get too heavy; there are too many of them; my love is too small; I even feel with terror, 'I have no love in my heart, I have nothing to give. . . .' And yet I have to pretend that I have. But strange and wonderful, the make-believe becomes true. If you will to love someone, you soon do. You will to love this cranky old man and someday you do. It depends on how hard you try."[1]

---

1. Robert Ellsberg, ed., *Dorothy Day: Selected Writings* (Maryknoll, NY: Orbis Books, 1992), 219.

Part I

Thistles and Figs

Mosaic of the Wedding at Cana,
Church of the Savior, Chora

Changing Course

ONE DAY JESUS ASKED the question, "Do people gather figs from thistles?" (Matthew 7:16). The answer is of course no—you harvest what you plant. Plant thistles and thistles take root and thistles they become. If you want to grow figs, you need to start with fig seeds. With this question, Jesus implicitly ridicules the idea that good can be brought about by evil means. Violence is not the means of creating a peaceful society. Vengeance does not pave the road to forgiveness. Spousal abuse does not lay the foundation for a lasting marriage. Rage is not a tool of reconciliation.

Yet, while figs do not grow from thistles, in the world of human choice and action, a positive change of attitude and direction is always a possibility. Sinners are the raw material of saints. The New Testament is crowded with accounts of transformations.

In the Church of the Savior in the Chora district of Istanbul, there is a fourteenth-century Byzantine mosaic that, in a single image, tells a story of an unlikely transformation: the conversion of water into wine for guests at a wedding feast in the village of Cana. In the background Jesus—his right hand extended in a gesture of blessing—stands side by side with his mother. In the foreground we see a servant pouring water from a smaller jug into a larger one. The water leaves the first jug a pale blue and tile by tile becomes a deep purple as it reaches the lip of the lower jug. "This, the first of his signs, Jesus did at Cana, in Galilee, and manifested his glory; and his disciples believed in him" (John 2:11).

This "first sign" that Jesus gave is a key to understanding everything in the Gospel. Jesus is constantly bringing about transformations: blind eyes to seeing eyes, withered limbs to working limbs, sickness into well-being, guilt into forgiveness, strangers into neighbors, enemies into friends, slaves into free people, armed men into disarmed men, crucifixion into resurrection, sorrow into joy, bread and wine into himself. Nature cannot produce figs from thistles, but God is doing this in our lives all the time. God's constant business in creation is making something out of nothing. As a Portuguese proverb declares, "God writes straight with crooked lines."

The convert Paul is an archetype of transformation. Paul, formerly a deadly adversary of Christ's followers, becomes Christ's apostle and his most tireless missionary, crisscrossing the Roman Empire, leaving behind him a trail of young churches that endure to this day. It was a miracle of enmity being turned to friendship, and it happened in a flash of time too small to measure, a sudden illumination. Witnessing the first deacon, Stephen, being stoned to death in Jerusalem must have been a key moment in setting the stage for Paul's conversion.

Peter is another man who made a radical about-face. Calling him away from his nets, Christ made the fisherman into a fisher of men. At the Garden of Gethsemane, the same Peter slashed the ear from one of those who had come to arrest Jesus. Far from commending Peter for his courage, Jesus healed the wound and commanded Peter to lay down his blood-stained weapon: "Put away your sword for whoever lives by the sword shall perish by the sword" (Matthew 26:42). For the remainder of his life, Peter was never again a threat to anyone's life, seeking only the conversion of opponents, never their death. Peter became a man who would rather die than kill.

How does such a conversion of heart take place? And what are the obstacles?

It was a question that haunted the Russian writer Leo Tolstoy, who for years struggled to turn from aristocrat to peasant, from rich man to poor man, from former soldier to peacemaker, though none of these intentions was ever fully achieved. As a child, Tolstoy was told by his older brother Nicholas that there was a green stick buried on their estate at the edge of a ravine in the ancient Zakaz forest. It was no ordinary piece of wood, said Nicholas. Carved into its surface were words "which would destroy all evil in the hearts of men and bring them everything good." Leo Tolstoy spent his entire life searching for the revelation. Even as an old man he wrote, "I still believe today that there is such a truth, that it will be revealed to all and will fulfill its promise."[1] Tolstoy is buried near the ravine in the Zakaz forest, the very place where he had sought the green stick.

Were we to discover it, my guess is that the green stick would probably turn out to bear a three-word sentence we have often read but have found so difficult that we have reburied it in a ravine within ourselves: "Love your enemies."

Twice in the Gospels, first in Matthew and then in Luke, Jesus is quoted on this remarkable teaching, unique to Christianity:

> *You have heard that it was said you shall love your neighbor and hate your enemy, but I say to you love your enemies and pray for those who persecute you, so that you may be children of your Father who is in heaven; for he makes his sun rise on the evil and on the good, and sends rain on the just and on the unjust. For if you love those who love you, what reward have you? Do not even tax collectors do the same?* (Matthew 5:43-46)

> *Love your enemies, do good to those who hate you, bless those who curse you, pray for those who abuse you. To him who strikes you on the cheek, offer the other also; and to him who takes away your cloak, do not withhold your coat as well. Give to everyone who begs from you; and of him who takes away your goods, do not ask them again. As you wish that others would do to you, do so to them.* (Luke 6:27-31)

Perhaps we Christians have heard these words too often to be stunned by their plain meaning, but to those who first heard Jesus, this teaching would have been astonishing and controversial. Few would have said "amen." Some would have shrugged their shoulders and muttered, "Love a Roman soldier? You're out of your mind." Zealots in the crowd would have considered such teaching traitorous, for all nationalisms thrive on enmity. Challenge nationalism, or

---

1. Henri Troyat, *Tolstoy* (Garden City, NY: Doubleday, 1967), 16.

speak against enmity in too specific a way, and you make enemies on the spot.

Nationalism is as powerful as an ocean tide. I recall an exchange during the question period following a talk opposing the Vietnam War that I gave in Milwaukee, Wisconsin, back in 1968. I had recently been involved in an act of war resistance that would soon result in my spending a year in prison, but for the moment I was free on bail. During the question period, an angry woman holding a small American flag stood up and challenged me to put my hand over my heart and recite the Pledge of Allegiance.[2] I said that flags ought not to be treated as idols and suggested instead that all of us rise and join in reciting the Our Father, which we did. Her anger seemed to recede a bit, but I suspect in her eyes I was a traitor. I had failed her patriotism test.

We tend to forget that the country in which Jesus entered history and gathered his first disciples was not the idyllic place Christmas cards have made of it, a quiet pastoral land populated with attractive sheep, colorfully dressed shepherds, and tidy villages crowning fertile hilltops. It was a country enduring military occupation in which most Jews suffered and where anyone perceived as a dissident was likely to be executed. In Roman-ruled Palestine, a naked Jew nailed to a cross was not an unfamiliar sight. To Jesus' first audience, enemies were numerous, ruthless, and close at hand.

Not only were there the Romans to hate, with their armies and idols, and emperor-gods. There were the enemies within Israel, not least the tax collectors who extorted as much money as they could, for their own pay was a percentage of the take. There were also Jews who were aping the Romans and Greeks, dressing—and undressing—as they did, all the while scrambling up the ladder, fraterniz-

---

2. "I pledge allegiance to the flag of the United States of America, and to the Republic for which it stands, one nation under God, indivisible, with liberty and justice for all." Sessions of the U.S. Congress begin with the recital of the pledge. It is also commonly recited in U.S. classrooms at the beginning of each school day, although the Supreme Court has ruled that students cannot be compelled to recite the pledge or be punished for not doing so.

ing and collaborating with the Roman occupiers. And even among those religious Jews trying to remain faithful to tradition, there were divisions about what was and was not essential in religious law and practice as well as heated arguments about how to relate to the Romans. A growing number of Jews, the Zealots, saw no solution but violent resistance. Some others, such as the ascetic Essenes, chose the strategy of monastic withdrawal; they lived in the desert near the Dead Sea where neither the Romans nor their collaborators often ventured.

No doubt Jesus also had Romans and Rome's agents listening to what he had to say, some out of curiosity, others because it was their job to listen. From the Roman point of view, the indigestible Jews, even if subdued, remained enemies. The Romans regarded this one-godded, statue-smashing, civilization-resisting people with amusement, bewilderment, and contempt—a people well deserving whatever lashes they received. Some of those lashes would have been delivered by the Romans in blind rage for having been stationed in this appalling, uncultured backwater. Judaea and Galilee were not sought-after postings for Roman soldiers—or for the Roman prefect at the time, Pontius Pilate.

Jesus was controversial. Not only were his teachings revolutionary, but the more respectable members of society were put off by the fact that many drawn to him were people who had lived scandalous lives: prostitutes, tax collectors, and even a Roman officer who begged Jesus to heal his servant. The Gospel says plainly that Jesus loved sinners, and that created scandal.

Many must have been impressed by his courage—no one accused Jesus of cowardice—but some would have judged him foolhardy, like a man putting his head in a lion's mouth. While Jesus refused to take up weapons or sanction their use, he kept no prudent silence and was anything but a collaborator. He did not hesitate to say and do things that made him a target. Perhaps the event that assured his crucifixion was what he did to the money-changers within the Temple precincts in Jerusalem. He made a whip of cords, something that stings but causes no wounds, and set the merchants running, meanwhile overturning their tables and scattering their coins (Matthew 21:12; Mark 11:15-18; Luke 19:45-48; and John 2:13-16). Anyone who disrupts business as usual will soon have enemies.

Many devout people were also dismayed by what seemed to them his careless religious practice, especially not keeping the Sabbath as strictly as many Pharisees thought Jews should. People were not made for the Sabbath, Jesus responded, but the Sabbath made for people (Mark 2:27). Zealots hated him both for not being a Zealot and for drawing away people who might have been recruited. Those who led the religious establishment were so incensed that they managed to arrange his execution, pointing out to the Romans that Jesus was a troublemaker who had been "perverting the nation" (Luke 23:2). It was the Romans who both tortured Jesus and carried out his execution.

Any Christian who believes Jesus to be God incarnate, the Second Person of the Holy Trinity, who entered history not by chance but purposefully, at an exact moment and chosen place, becoming fully human as the child of the Virgin Mary, will find it worthwhile to think about the Incarnation happening just then, not in peaceful times but in a humiliated, over-taxed land governed by brutal, bitterly resented occupation troops. Jesus was born, lived, crucified, and rose from the dead in a land of extreme enmity.

Transposing Gospel events into our own world and time, many of us would find ourselves alarmed and shocked by the things Jesus said and did, for actions that seem admirable in an ancient narrative might be judged unwise and untimely, if not insane, if they occurred in equivalent circumstances here and now. Love our enemies? Does that mean loving criminals, murderers, and terrorists? Call on people to get rid of their weapons? Apprentice ourselves to a man who fails to say a patriotic word or wave a single flag? Many would say such a man had no one to blame for his troubles but himself.

It was a big step, and a risky one, to become one of his disciples. Had you lived in Judaea or Galilee when the events recorded in the Gospel were happening, are you sure you would have wanted to be identified with him?

What Does It Mean to Love?

Whoever hates his brother is a murderer.
—1 John 3:15

NOWHERE IN THE GOSPELS does Christ instruct us to hate our enemies—instead we are told to love them. But if we are going to take seriously the command to love our enemies, it would help to know what Christ means, and doesn't mean, by love.

In ordinary usage the word "love" has mainly to do with feelings—positive emotional bonds or longings or likings, from the trivial to the sublime: "I love the pizzas they make at Danilo's." "I love Woody Allen films." "I'm madly in love with [insert a name]." Lovemaking usually means sexual intercourse, an action that may or may not have anything to do with love.

Along these lines the *American Heritage Dictionary* defines love as an "intense affection and warm feeling for another person; strong sexual desire for another person; a strong fondness or enthusiasm."

Such a definition makes Christ's commandment to love one's enemies incomprehensible. We can safely say that even Jesus was without intense affection or warm feelings for his judges, torturers, and executioners. Yet he loved them.

The *Oxford English Dictionary* provides both a less emotional and more biblical definition:

Love . . . [is that] disposition or state of feeling with regard to a person which . . . manifests itself in solicitude for the welfare of the object. . . . [Love is] applied in an eminent sense to the paternal benevolence and affection of God toward His children, to the affectionate devotion directed to God from His creatures, and to the

13

*affection of one created being to another so far as it is prompted by
the sense of their common relationship to God.*

As used in the Bible, love has first of all to do with action and
responsibility, not about your emotions or liking someone. To
love is to do what you can to provide for the well-being of another
whether you like that person or not. In explaining his Father's love,
Jesus talks not about sentiments but about what God gives and does:
"Your Father in heaven who makes the sun rise on the evil and on
the good, and sends rain on the just and the unjust" (Matthew 6:45).

An act of love may be animated by a sense of gratitude and delight
in someone else—wonderful when it happens—or it may be done
despite exhaustion, depression, fear, aversion, or anger; it may be
done simply as an obedient response to Christ's teaching; it may be
done as a prayer and a response to God who is our common creator,
who links us all, in whose image each of us is made, in whom we are
brothers and sisters, who has bound together love of God with love
of neighbor.

Think of an exhausted parent awoken at three in the morning by a
crying infant who, even after being held and fed, its diaper changed,
carried and stroked and sung to, refuses to stop crying. It's not a time
when one feels grateful for the child or glad to be alive. Ignoring
irritated feelings, you do what is needed and try to do it gently and
patiently. This is an image of actual love.

As my friend Dana Mills-Powell says, "First act in love—your
feelings will follow."

In the final analysis love has little to do with moods, affections,
or affinities. "Our job is to love others without stopping to inquire
whether or not they are worthy," Thomas Merton wrote in *Disputed
Questions*. "That is not our business and, in fact, it is nobody's business. What we are asked to do is to love, and this love itself will ren-
der both ourselves and our neighbors worthy."[1]

To become even vaguely aware of each person being a bearer of

---

1. Thomas Merton, "The Power and Meaning of Love," in Thomas Merton,
Disputed Questions (New York: Farrar, Straus & Cudahy), 125.

the divine image helps open the door to love. According to Saint Paul, the greatest gifts of God are faith, hope, and love, and of these three the most important is love. Describing the qualities of love, Paul says nothing about emotions, only that love is patient and kind, without jealousy or boasting, without arrogance or rudeness, doesn't insist on having its own way, doesn't rejoice at wrong but rather in the right, and endures everything (1 Corinthians 13:4-13).

In his love Jesus has united us to himself, Paul wrote to the church in Corinth, making us into "ambassadors of Christ" called to undertake "the ministry of reconciliation" (2 Corinthians 5:17-20).

But what is reconciliation? This is a word rarely used in daily conversation. It means the restoration of relationships whose brokenness, like a smashed plate, seems beyond repair. Think of healing. Reconciliation is the healing of our deepest social wounds, whether within a fractured marriage or between nations. The biblical meaning of reconciliation has to do with relationships transformed in the peace of God. The current of reconciliation is love, without which the healing of damaged relationships is impossible. Events in the process of reconciliation mark the way toward "the holy mountain" of Isaiah's prophecy where "the lion and the lamb shall dwell together . . . and a little child shall lead them" (Isaiah 11:1-9).

Reconciliation was the great dream of Martin Luther King Jr. In his most famous sermon he proclaimed, "I have a dream that one day on the red hills of Georgia, sons of former slaves and sons of former slave-owners will be able to sit down together at the table of brotherhood. . . . I have a dream today!"[2]

Reconciliation is not only a word describing what could happen in the future but also is a reality that already exists, if only we open our eyes a little wider. Even now, despite all our fractured relationships, we are in fact profoundly interconnected and interdependent. None of us could live without the help of countless others near and far, present and past, friend and foe. Everything we have, not only

---

2. Speech given at the March on Washington in 1963, see James Washington, ed., *A Testament of Hope: The Essential Writings of Martin Luther King* (New York: Harper & Row, 1986), 217.

material things, but our words, our ideas, our skills, our faith, the music and stories that give courage, understanding and that delight the heart—everything we have has been given to us by others. There is a hidden wholeness. Our basic unity, existing beneath all divisions, has to do with each of us being bearers of the divine image. "We are already one," said Thomas Merton a few weeks before his death, "but we imagine that we are not. What we have to recover is our original unity."[3]

---

3. Thomas Merton, "Monastic Experience and East–West Dialogue," *The Asian Journal of Thomas Merton* (New York: New Directions, 1973), 309-17.

Who Is My Enemy?

THE WORDS "ENEMY" and "enmity" come from the Latin, *inimicus*. *Amicus* means friend. Add the negative prefix *in* and change the *a* in *amicus* to *i* and you get *inimicus*. Defined broadly, an enemy is the opposite of a friend.

My son Daniel, when he was seven, offered a very crisp definition of what it is to be a nonfriend when he told another boy to "go away and drop dead." In the plain speech of childhood, an enemy is someone, anyone, who would do well to go away and drop dead.

The *Oxford English Dictionary* gives a more elegant definition. An enemy, it says, is an "unfriendly or hostile person, one that cherishes hatred, and who works to do ill to another."

This is an astute entry as it points the finger not only toward another person or nation but also at oneself. We are used to perceiving others as enemies, never ourselves. But if I am unfriendly or hostile toward others, if I cherish hatred or participate in doing ill to others, or even if I am busy threatening or preparing to do ill, I have made myself into an enemy. Unless I make a break with enmity, the enemy of my enemy is me. If I wish to break the cycle of enmity, I had better keep in mind that the only enemy over whom I have much influence is myself.

Aleksandr Solzhenitsyn, longtime captive in the Soviet chain of prison camps called the Gulag, discovered while a prisoner that the line of enmity ran not between himself and his adversary but through his and every human heart:

> If only it were all so simple! If only there were evil people somewhere insidiously committing evil deeds and it were necessary only to separate them from the rest of us and destroy them. But the dividing

line between good and evil cuts through the heart of every human being, and who is willing to destroy a piece of his own heart?[1]

Who of us can claim to have a heart entirely free of evil? Who of us isn't someone's enemy? And even an enemy of one's self? Gandhi, the prophet of nonviolence who played a crucial role in India's struggle for independence, made a similar remark: "I have only three enemies. My favorite enemy, the one most easily influenced for the better, is the British nation. My second enemy, the Indian people, is far more difficult to influence. But my most formidable opponent is a man named Mohandas K. Gandhi. With him I seem to have very little influence." Pogo, an affable American cartoon character whose strip flourished in the 1950s, put it in even fewer words: "We have met the enemy and he is us." The enemy we encounter most often is seen not through the window but in the mirror.

But of course there are also the enemies we *have* rather than the enemies we *are*.

An enemy is anyone I feel threatened by and seek to defend myself against. An enemy is a person or group of people whose defeat I would count a victory. What for them would be bad news for me would be good news. An enemy is someone whose death I would not mourn and might even welcome and celebrate, as did many Americans and others when Osama bin Laden was killed.

Enemies can be divided into two broad categories, those nearby and those far away—those known by name and those who are strangers.

As any judge or policeman will tell you, most murders and other acts of abuse and violence occur between people who know each other—a member of one's family, a friend, a neighbor, a co-worker. When a wife or husband is killed, at the top of the list of suspects is the spouse. Take away all the court cases involving intrafamily disputes and thousands of lawyers and judges would be out of work.

The list of enemies includes those I know by name as well as people I see in terms of categories and stereotypes: blacks, whites, Muslims,

---

1. Aleksandr Solzhenitsyn, *The Gulag Archipelago,* vol. 2, "The Ascent," trans. Thomas P. Whitney (New York: Harper & Row, 1974).

Arabs, Jews, Asians, gays, punks, pro-abortionists, pro-lifers. . . . The list can zigzag on for miles. It may well include people in political groups in opposition to my own or people in important roles of political leadership whose views and actions I detest. It is hard to imagine a president or prime minister who would dare appear in public without bodyguards. Assassins are mainly homegrown.

Then there are the distant enemies. Internationally, an enemy is a mass of people I am encouraged, even required, to perceive as a threat to my nation and may, in case of war, even be required to kill or whose killing I would regard as necessary, if not good—or, in the case of noncombatants, as an unfortunate consequence of a just war. Such enemies are not acquired through personal animosity but simply because of their birth and nationality. The enemy in such cases is not an individual but an entire people defined by national borders or ideology.

Such enmity is remarkably impersonal and flexible—last year's mortal enemy can become this year's ally. For Americans in the middle of the twentieth century the principal enemies were Germany, Italy, and Japan, today all allies. Next came the Soviet Union, an ally during the war with Hitler's Third Reich, the arch-foe for half a century following that war, today no longer an enemy but also not quite a friend. During the decades of the Cold War (1947-1991), we in the West were collectively prepared for war with Russians, and Russians for war with the West. On the U.S. side, nuclear-armed B-52 bombers were in the air twenty-four hours a day, while nuclear-tipped missiles stood constantly ready for launch.[2] In fact, even in the post–Cold War world, a vast array of weapons of mass destruction is still poised for use.

In the post–9/11 world, we find ourselves with a borderless enemy whom we sometimes describe as "Islamicists" or "jihadists." The "War on Terror," a term coined by George W. Bush, has led the United States and its allies into lengthy wars in Iraq and Afghanistan, with the Afghan war currently extending into Pakistan, Yemen, and Somalia. There is both overt and covert engagement with "jihadists" in a number of other countries.

---

2. For a detailed account of how close we came to nuclear war, see Eric Schlosser, *Command and Control: Nuclear Weapons, the Damascus Accident, and the Illusion of Safety* (New York: Penguin, 2013).

Political speeches, blog content, movies, and spy fiction all serve to develop and reinforce enemy stereotypes so that little by little one can regard an entire nation or category of people as an appropriate target of war. News reports emphasize war crimes committed by the enemy while ignoring or playing down the war crimes "our side" commits—for example, the many noncombatant deaths caused by pilotless drones are rarely headline news in the Western press.

A fortune beyond the reach of imagination is expended on the destruction not merely of particular rulers with whom we are at odds but the devastation of whole towns and cities. The casualties are mainly the most vulnerable people, the very young, the very old, the very ill, those least able to survive. Most of those killed are in reality *not* the enemy.

Occasionally we encounter an enemy face to face and discover a friend. A much-decorated American veteran of World War II tells a story of his unexpected encounter with a German soldier:

> My name is Jack Leroy Tueller. This is two weeks after D-Day [June 6, 1944]. It's dark, raining, muddy, and I'm stressed, so I get my trumpet out and the commander says: "Jack, don't play tonight, because there is one sniper left." But I thought to myself that German sniper is as scared and lonely as I am. So I thought, I'll play his love song ["Lili Marleen," a popular German romantic song]. The next morning, here comes a jeep from up the beach about a mile and a half away, and the military police says: "Hey captain, there's some German prisoners getting ready to go to England. One of them keeps saying in broken English, 'Who played that trumpet last night?'" I met the boy and he burst into sobs. He said, "When I heard that number that you played, I thought about my fiancé in Germany, I thought about my mother and dad, about my brothers and sisters, and I couldn't fire." And he stuck out his hand, and I shook the hand of the enemy. He was no enemy. He was scared and lonely like me.[3]

---

3. http://www.youtube.com/watch?v=aQzRxGuBnok.

The Gospel according to John Wayne

ONE OF THE UNIQUE ASPECTS of being human is the role stories play in our lives and have played as far back as the threads of human memory lead us. Stories inspire, enlighten, connect, delight, warn, terrify, admonish, and surprise. We need them with an urgency that resembles hunger. Not merely entertainment, stories can save lives or play a part in turning us into killers.

In 1955, when I was thirteen, I went to the Museum of Modern Art in New York to see a photo exhibition that has haunted me ever since. Its theme was "The Family of Man." The curator, Edward Steichen, brought together a vast sequence of photos that not only asserted but demonstrated that, for all the diversity of culture, skin color, local economy and development, varieties of religion, and differences of clothing, we are indeed one human family bound together in love, pain, labor, awe, anger, gratitude, and death. I bought the exhibition book[1] and still have it despite many moves, returning to it ever since as if it were a Bible without words. Taken as a whole, the collection of photos has as its golden thread the radical *us-ness* of being. It has helped me better understand that beneath our separateness is our unity. It's about the "our" in the Our Father.

Among the book's images that I especially love is one of an old African storyteller in a fire-illuminated hut. We see him at the top of a circle of young people, boys and girls who are listening to the old man with absolute attention and wonder. The storyteller's eyes are wide open, his mouth a perfect O, his eyebrows arched high into his forehead, his hands raised above his head, all ten fingers outstretched. If he were telling the tale of Sleeping Beauty, the dream-

---

1. Edward Steichen, *The Family of Man* (New York: Museum of Modern Art; distributed by Harry N. Abrams, 1955).

ing princess would just be waking up. If he were telling the story of Jesus' life, this might be the moment when the disciples discover the empty tomb.

The photo is an icon of the power of storytelling.

"In traditional African cultures, not even the chief or the healer is as important as the storyteller," Joseph Donders, a Dutch priest who had spent much of his life in Africa, once told me. "The survival of the tribe from generation to generation depends on stories, only the stories have to reveal truth. With truth-revealing stories the storyteller becomes the guardian not only of his actual audience but of those not yet born. This is because, in times of crisis, people are guided not by theories or principles but by stories. True stories are life saving; false stories lead toward disaster. Stories are proven true by the test of time. An old story that has been told for centuries and has been tested in many times of crisis can be regarded as true."

"The testing of stories," Donders added, "requires the passage of many generations. In fact two thousand years is about right."

Our conversation led us to consider the question of what was the most basic story in the modern world. We quickly agreed that it's not the Gospels of Matthew, Mark, Luke, and John. Rather, in its purest form, it's the Western movie. We decided to call it the Gospel according to John Wayne. (Our point of reference was not the off-

John Wayne in
Born to the West

camera John Wayne, who may have been as nonviolent as Gandhi, but John Wayne the actor in the gunslinger roles he often played.)

At the core of the Gospel according to John Wayne is a good man with a gun killing bad men with guns.

In its most classic version, it's the story of men who are evil to their core threatening decent people in a newly settled town in the lawless West in which there is a battered saloon and brothel at one end of the street and a newly painted church and schoolhouse at the other. Endangered by pathological killers, the well-being of the townspeople depends on the courage of one brave man and those, if any, whom he is able to rally behind him. While the film's ultimate battle has many variations, the iconic scene is the gunfight on Main Street—one man with a gun facing another man with a gun and both pulling the trigger.

There is sometimes a prefatory scene before the shoot-out in which we see the reluctant hero open a drawer and grasp his revolver, a weapon he had once put away with the fervent hope of never using it again. He is not, such scenes make clear, a man of violence, but now there is no alternative. He straps on his holster, inserts six bullets in the gun's chambers, and walks out the door knowing he may be dead within the hour. But in fact he survives. Goodness triumphs. It's the man who loves killing whose day ends in a coffin.

The story needn't be set in the Old West. The core elements adjust to any setting: rural or urban, past, present, or a Star Wars future where distances are measured in light years. The Gospel according to John Wayne is also the Gospel according to Luke Skywalker and the Gospel according to Batman. The moral is the same in any case: We are saved by deadly weapons plus the courage and skill of those community defenders who wield them.

It's far from an ignoble story or without elements of truth. There is real courage in it—the readiness of an honorable man to risk his life to protect his defenseless neighbors from wicked men whose death we who watch the film cannot help but wish for and, once it happens, welcome. If only briefly, it seems the world has been made a safer place.

The big problem with the Gospel according to John Wayne is that it hides from us the troubling fact that there is no such thing as a completely evil person—also the equally uncomfortable fact that not one of us is a completely good person.

Few biblical texts have more profound implications than this passage in the first chapter of Genesis:

> *God created man in his own image, in the image of God he created him; male and female he created them.* (Genesis 1:27)

If so, then there are no bad seeds. Our DNA does not oblige any of us to become murderers. No matter how damaged a person becomes in the process of growing up and entering adulthood, all of us are born bearing the divine image and can never entirely lose it.

For John of Kronstadt, one of the Russian saints of the nineteenth century, to become aware of this was one of the main challenges of Christian life. "Never confuse the person," he said, "formed in the image of God, with the evil that is in him, because evil is but a chance misfortune, illness, a devilish reverie. But the very essence of the person is the image of God, and this remains in him despite every disfigurement." Saint John's insight was not developed at a safe distance from the rough side of life—he was parish priest in Kronstadt, a port city with thousands of sailors and more than its share of drunkenness, crime, and violence of every kind. Many of his parishioners could be found in jail cells.

Like most ordinary Russians at the time, Saint John of Kronstadt avoided dehumanizing labels for men who had been convicted of criminal actions. Criminals and those in prison were instead commonly referred to as "unfortunates," a word packed with compassion. It was this attitude that helps explain why so few executions occurred in prerevolutionary Russia. Those who were convicted of murder and other grave crimes were instead sent to labor camps in Siberia.

The inability to see Christ in the other is the most common form of Christian spiritual blindness, as one of the prominent saints of the fourth century, John Chrysostom, often stressed. "If you fail to recognize Christ in the beggar outside the church door," he said, "you will not find Christ in the chalice." Or as Dorothy Day put it, "Those who do not see Christ in the poor are atheists indeed." Or as Thomas

Merton wrote, "Guard the image of man for it is the image of God."[2]

Yet the Gospel according to John Wayne remains a compelling story—the brave lone man who puts himself in the line of fire and kills a human monster (so he has been portrayed) whose death is a blessing for every honest person. The moral is always the same: The community can be protected only by the good killing the bad, or at the very least locking them up for the rest of their lives.

In the latter part of *Gone with the Wind*, a film that presents slavery as having been not so bad and with the wrong side winning the Civil War, the heroine, Scarlett O'Hara, returns to her family plantation, Tara, after the defeat of the South. Scarlett finds the mansion intact though the crops have been burned, her mother has died of typhoid, her father is insane with grief, her two sisters are ill, and most of the formerly happy slaves have ungratefully run off. Forced to take up labor that in better days had been done by slaves, Scarlett's life now centers on reviving the plantation through blood, sweat, and tears, even if the paradise that the Tara plantation once had been for her is lost indeed. When a drunken Yankee soldier arrives and is poised to rape her, Scarlett stands on the mansion's grand curved staircase, revolver hidden behind her back, then, at the last moment raises the weapon and shoots him in the face. Afterward, in shock, she says to her sister-in-law, "I've done murder." To her credit and the credit of the storytellers, Scarlett uses a razor-sharp word, murder, that doesn't mask what she has done. After pulling the trigger and seeing at close range the death she has caused, perhaps Scarlett realizes she might have aimed at the man's legs and protected herself without becoming a murderer.

How rare is the movie in which the hero or heroine is allowed to aim for the legs or, rarer still, find a bullet-free, nonviolent solution. In film after film, the implicit message is that, in confrontations with evil, there are no nonlethal—still less nonviolent—solutions. It's a kill-or-be-killed world. Period. Next subject.

---

2. Thomas Merton, *Raids on the Unspeakable* (New York: New Directions, 1966), 6.

The Story of the Merciful Enemy

CHRISTIANITY, SHAPED as it is by the Gospels of Matthew, Mark, Luke, and John, provides a very different narrative than the Gospel according to John Wayne. Christ's basic message is that we are saved not by weapons and the killing of adversaries but by conversion and love—a tough, unsentimental love that extends even to our enemies. The four Gospels provide an anthology of stories, each of which has to do with self-giving love.

In one of these Jesus is asked by a lawyer, "What must I do to inherit eternal life?" (Luke 10:25-37). For anyone who has ever longed for a life beyond death, or for experiences of the kingdom of God even in this present life, what question could be more important?

Jesus thought this was something that any Jew should be able to answer, certainly a lawyer expert in the Mosaic texts. "What is written in the law?" he asked. "How do you read it?"

The lawyer responded, "You shall love the Lord your God with all your heart, and with all your soul, and with all your strength, and with all your mind; and your neighbor as yourself."

"You have answered correctly," Jesus told him. "Do this, and you will live."

Then came the lawyer's real question, one he could not answer for himself: "And who is my neighbor?"

Jesus responds with a story of a lone man who is attacked and savagely beaten while walking along that road that leads from the heights of Jerusalem down to the ancient city of Jericho near the River Jordan. Everything is taken from the victim, even his clothing. His assailants leave him half-dead.

The story has been so often told that even those who are biblically illiterate are likely to know what followed: A priest and a Levite, two fellow Jews of high status in Israel's theocratic society, pass by the injured man "on the other side of the road." We can almost hear them talking about how dangerous it is to travel these days, even with all these Roman soldiers around.

Then along comes a man riding a donkey. No name is given. We know nothing biographical about him except the fact that he is a Samaritan. The Samaritans were despised cousins of the Jews, who were regarded with hostility because their faith did not center on Jerusalem and its temple. Though Samaritans were also committed to the Law of Moses, within Judaea they were regarded as heretics and treated as enemies.

The crucial thing about the Samaritan, says Jesus, is that he "had compassion." He sees the injured man and cannot avert his eyes and turn his back on him. He pours oil and wine on the man's wounds. Putting the stranger on his donkey, the Samaritan then takes him to an inn where he pays the innkeeper to do everything he can for the man, promising more money if needed the next time he passes by.

"Who is my neighbor?" Having listened to the story, the questioner recognizes that it's the man who showed mercy even though he happens to be a reviled outsider. The Samaritan set aside his plans, inconvenienced himself, spent his money, and committed himself to saving the life of someone whom he had never met but who awakened his compassion. The result was that an injured stranger, someone he might have labeled an enemy, became his guest.

Jesus says to the lawyer, and to us as well, "Go and do likewise."

It's such a simple story! It's quickly told, with an easy-to-grasp message. If by some calamity every copy of the New Testament were destroyed but the parable of the Good Samaritan survived, the parable would serve as a grain-sized summary of the Gospels' insistence that love of God is impossible without love of neighbor.

Yet even committed Christians find it hard to translate the parable into their own lives. I think of an experiment done in the 1950s at Princeton University in New Jersey.

A number of theological students were asked to prepare sermons on the parable of the Good Samaritan. These were to be taped for

grading by a professor of homiletics. It seemed an ordinary assign-
ment, but those responsible for the project were less interested in
what the aspiring pastors would say about the parable than in how
the story shaped their response to others in need.

Without their knowledge, the students had been divided into several groups. Some were called on a certain morning and told that
they could come to the taping room any time in the day. Those in the
second group were told that they had to be there within the next few
hours. The rest were to be told that an error had been made—they
should have been called with their appointment time the day before
but a mistake had been made; they should come without delay—the
person recording the sermon was waiting.

The testers had arranged that the students, as they arrived at
the building where the sermons were being recorded, would pass
by someone, apparently unconscious, slumped in a doorway, not a
common sight on the campus of Ivy League Princeton.

What were the results? Carrying the manuscripts of compelling
sermons on the parable of the Good Samaritan, barely a third took
the time to stop and find out if the person in the doorway needed
help. Those who did stop were mainly students who had been told
they could come whenever they wished. The sense of having time
gave them time to notice, time for a caring response, time to become
a neighbor, time to be a Good Samaritan. They didn't feel trapped in
the rush hour of deadlines, the constant problem of so many people,
not least clergy, which perhaps is why Jesus cast a priest and Levite
in those unfortunate roles in his parable.

In explanation, no doubt many of the students who failed to
stop said, "But I had no time!" In reality, as opposed to our perception of reality, the day is not a prison of schedules and deadlines.
In reality each student had just as much time as any other, but for
many of them the *sense* of being on deadline narrowed their vision
of the world around them. In addition, for all the students there was
the enemy factor: this inert person shouldn't be there and—who
knows?—he might be dangerous.

We too have time. When we have to choose between a neighbor

in need and our schedule for the day, somehow we have to learn to let the former take priority. "The gate of heaven is everywhere,"[1] the Trappist monk Thomas Merton pointed out, the catch being that we have to take time to notice the gate and open it. Most of the time the gate of heaven is another human being, and even someone who might pose a threat.

The sense of having time, or not having it, isn't simply a matter of having a full or empty calendar. Sometimes people who lead the most demanding, complicated lives manage to drop everything and respond, like the Good Samaritan, to the unexpected as if there was nothing else that mattered, aware that it's often in unplanned and unwanted events that God breaks into our lives. A life too imprisoned in plans causes blindness. "Life is what happens after you plan it," we often say in my family. Never let your plans blind you to those around you.

I recall an experience I had during the late sixties when I was accompanying Thich Nhat Hanh, a Vietnamese Buddhist monk and teacher of mindfulness who was visiting the United States. He was about to give a lecture at the University of Michigan on the war in Vietnam and also read aloud some of his poetry. Waiting for the elevator doors to open, I noticed my brown-robed companion gazing at the clock above the elevator doors. Pointing to the clock, he said to me, "You know, Jim, a few hundred years ago it would not have been a clock, it would have been a crucifix."

How many people have been unable to follow the example of the Good Samaritan because they glanced at their watch and realized they just didn't have time?

---

1. Thomas Merton, *Conjectures of a Guilty Bystander* (New York: Doubleday, 1966), 142.

A Cathedral Builder's Sense of Time

OVERCOMING ENMITY requires a larger sense of time.

In the town where I grew up—Red Bank, New Jersey—there were many churches, some as imposing as banks, others more modest. As a child I was impressed with how different the church buildings were. Only later did I realize how much they had in common, including the fact that not one of the churches had been standing for as much as a century. To find something really old, at least old by American standards, you had to go a few miles south, to Shrewsbury, where several buildings dated back to colonial times.

On one corner of Shrewsbury's main intersection stood Christ Episcopal Church, the sideboards of which had been scarred by musket balls fired in 1778 during the Revolutionary War, and the pews inside the church were still faintly stained—at least so it seemed to me—with the blood of men wounded in the Battle of Monmouth.

Directly across the street was another old structure, the Quaker Meeting House, barn sized and stunningly plain, the long wooden benches inside engulfed in the building's impressive silence.

These older places of worship within biking range of our house expanded my sense of time quite a bit, but when I thought of the ancient churches on the other side of the Atlantic Ocean, photos of which I had seen in an encyclopedia at school, even the oldest church I knew about in America seemed almost new.

As an adult, when my work with several peace groups began to bring me to Europe, nothing impressed me more than the great cathedrals. Now I live just a minute's walk from one of them, the oldest surviving building in the Dutch city of Alkmaar. Its construction began in 1470, twenty-two years before Columbus's first voyage to the New World, and was completed half a century later.

Chartres Cathedral

For me, perhaps the most astonishing cathedral in western Europe is Our Lady of Chartres, southwest of Paris, to which I've returned repeatedly. It amazes me not only that such a place exists and has survived the storms of history but that human beings ever imagined enclosing space in this vast envelope of carefully balanced stone and glass. The skyscrapers in New York are awe inspiring but make you feel insignificant, while Chartres makes you feel, if not significant as an individual, then significant as a human being. Chartres, like so many other ancient churches, reminds me of the famous sentence from Dostoevsky: "The world will be saved by beauty."

One day, standing on the roof of Chartres, I realized that the people who had undertaken the building of the great cathedrals had a very different sense of time than I did. In the modern world even the tallest structures are normally built in a matter of months or, at most, a year or two. But the people who laid the foundation of Chartres in the twelfth century knew they would be long dead before the work they were part of was finished. They knew they would spend the rest of their lives doing hard labor, cutting stone, lifting it up, putting it in place, ending each day exhausted, working with ever more risk as the walls rose up, and finally in their graves long before the building was roofed. Perhaps their children or their grandchildren would see the finished church.

Our modern high-technology culture rarely prepares us to think about spending our entire life doing something that is profoundly worthwhile but won't be completed in our lifetime. We don't have a cathedral builder's sense of time.

It isn't just that we are in a hurry in putting up buildings; we tend to be in a rush about everything. Those of us who are drawn to some aspect of peacemaking can even be in a hurry about peacemaking. I recall that during the Vietnam War, a study showed that the average period of involvement in antiwar struggle was six months.

It's amazing I didn't burn out, though I came close to that state several times. Thomas Merton was addressing my frustrations at how slow and ineffective was the peace work I was engaged in when he sent me a letter about detachment and perseverance. It included this passage:

> *The big results are not in your hands or mine, but they suddenly happen, and we can share in them; but there is no point in building our lives on this personal satisfaction, which may be denied us and which after all is not that important. . . . The real hope . . . is not in something we think we can do but in God who is making something good out of it in some way we cannot see. If we can do His will, we will be helping in this process. But we will not necessarily know all about it beforehand.*[1]

---

1. Letter from Thomas Merton to Jim Forest dated February 21, 1966; the full text is published in Thomas Merton, *The Hidden Ground of Love,* ed. William Shannon (New York: Farrar, Straus & Giroux, 1985), 294-97.

Merton's letter helped me get through a difficult period and keep going. The times were daunting—it was impossible not to be discouraged. The Vietnam War was getting worse by the day, the number of casualties was rising steadily, young Americans who could not have found Vietnam on a world map were being drafted by the thousands, and the efforts being made by antiwar groups like the one I was then part of (the Catholic Peace Fellowship) seemed to be having no impact. But in fact, as one sees looking back, the impact of those opposing the war was considerable. Though it took nearly a decade for the war to come to its sudden end in 1975, the fact that a growing percentage—ultimately a majority—of the American public opposed the war helped prevent such acts of destruction as bombing the dike system of North Vietnam, a plan that would have meant death by drowning for vast numbers of people.

The main work the Catholic Peace Fellowship was engaged in was letting draft-age Catholics know that conscientious objection was an option, to make known the tradition of war resistance from the early church onward, and to publicize what recent popes and the Second Vatican Council had to say about conscience and war.[2] For all the frustrations we faced, the work we were a part of helps explain the remarkable fact that, during the Vietnam War, 170,000 young Americans (a large percentage of them Catholics) were granted conscientious objector deferments and performed alternative service. Thousands more moved to Canada or other countries. Many went to prison.

We achieved too little but we also achieved a great deal. If we failed to build a cathedral, at least we erected a chapel.

---

2. Not only did the Council support conscientious objection but declared orders that conflict with the "all-embracing principles of natural law" to be criminal, stating further that "blind obedience cannot excuse those who yield to them," and that "the courage of those who fearlessly and openly resist such commands merits supreme commendation" (*Gaudium et spes*, Constitution on the Church in the Modern World, no. 79).

Eyes Wide Open

ANOTHER OF THE GOSPELS' basic stories is the recognition of Christ at Emmaus, an account of the Resurrection told with considerable detail.

For some years I was part of the Emmaus community in New York, a house of hospitality whose guests included runaways and ex-prisoners. It could also have been called a house of bread for strangers, a house of free meals, a house of interruptions. We had a steady flow of guests, many of whom were not expected. People often slept on the living-room couch and in sleeping bags rolled out on the living-room floor. We always had too much to do and too many guests, each with special needs.

One day a visiting artist, Barbara Loste, drew a black-line picture of sliced bread on our living-room wall. Big black letters surrounded the image with the text of the Emmaus story. Barbara's drawing and calligraphy could not be ignored. Silently or aloud, alone and communally, we read the words so often that probably any of us could have recited much of the narrative by heart:

> *That very day two of them were going to a village named Emmaus, about seven miles from Jerusalem, and talking with each other about all these things that had happened. While they were talking and discussing together, Jesus himself drew near and went with them. But their eyes were kept from recognizing him. And he said to them, "What is this conversation which you are holding with each other as you walk?" And they stood still, looking sad. Then one of them, named Cleopas, answered him, "Are you the only visitor to Jerusalem who does not know the things that have happened there in these days?" And he said to them, "What things?" And they said to him, "Concerning Jesus of Nazareth, who was a prophet mighty*

in deed and word before God and all the people, and how our chief priests and rulers delivered him up to be condemned to death, and crucified him. But we had hoped that he was the one to redeem Israel. Yes, and besides all this, it is now the third day since this happened. Moreover, some women of our company amazed us. They were at the tomb early in the morning and did not find his body; and they came back saying that they had even seen a vision of angels, who said that he was alive. Some of those who were with us went to the tomb, and found it just as the women had said; but him they did not see." And he said to them, "O foolish men, and slow of heart to believe all that the prophets have spoken! Was it not necessary that the Christ should suffer these things and enter into his glory?" And beginning with Moses and all the prophets, he interpreted to them in all the scriptures the things concerning himself. So they drew near to the village to which they were going. He appeared to be going further, but they constrained him, saying, "Stay with us, for it is toward evening and the day is now far spent." So he went in to stay with them. When he was at table with them, he took the bread and blessed, and broke it, and gave it to them. And their eyes were opened and they recognized him; and he vanished out of their sight. They said to each other, "Did not our hearts burn within us while he talked to us on the road, while he opened to us the scriptures?" And they rose that same hour and returned to Jerusalem. (Luke 24:13-35)

One consequence of our frequent immersion in the Emmaus text was that everyone involved with the community developed a deep sense of identification with the two disciples in Luke's story and their initial inability to see whom they were with.

The Emmaus story is all about seeing—and failing to see.

We meet the two disciples in a state of near blindness caused by grief and disillusionment, their attention focused on the road and their sandals. Along the way they are joined by—so it seems to them—a stranger. The unrecognized Jesus then speaks to them at length, interpreting the sacred texts concerning the Messiah—himself—from Moses to the prophets. Still there is no recognition. For them Jesus is dead, the executioners are still in charge. The money-changers have repaired their tables in the Temple and are back in business.

The uninvited stranger had attached himself to the two disciples, but when they reach Emmaus it is they who press him to stay. On the road, "their eyes were kept from recognizing him," writes Luke, but at the table in Emmaus, they are given a clarity of sight they had never known before in their lives. "He took bread and blessed it, and broke it, and gave it to them. And their eyes were opened and they recognized him . . . they knew him in the breaking of bread."

Perhaps what finally made the difference was noticing the bread breaker's wounded hands.

At Emmaus House, where we daily broke bread with strangers, we learned the simplest truth of faith, the truth at the heart of the Emmaus narrative: Christian life is the continual struggle to see the face of Jesus in those around us—and sometimes it happens.

Etching by Rembrandt, Meal at Emmaus

Suddenly, when we least expect it, a word is said, an expression alters an unexplored face, we glimpse beauty in someone we regarded with irritation, and the two-dimensional ideas we had concerning that other person are demolished. We find ourselves in the presence of a huge mystery. That person had seemed so easily mapped and labeled, so flat, so unsurprising, a kind of wallpaper, yet in the blink of an eye a seam is revealed, a door swings opens, and we find ourselves in Christ's presence.

I recall one nearly suicidal boy from Pennsylvania—call him Eric—who somehow found his way to Emmaus House after several days sleeping in bus stations. He had shoulder-length, red-tinged golden hair. He might have stepped out of a Botticelli painting of a fifteenth-century Florentine youth. Eric's father had ordered him out of the house until he submitted to getting "a normal haircut." In fact, more than a haircut was at issue. Father and son were bitterly at odds on many subjects. One issue was the war then going on in Vietnam, which the father supported and his son passionately opposed. They often found themselves shouting at each other and slamming doors. Finally the house had no room for both father and son.

While staying with us, just before breakfast one morning, Eric leaned backward over the kitchen stove, unaware that an open flame was burning under a tea kettle behind him, and his hair caught fire. We managed quickly to extinguish the flames, but by then Eric's upper back as well as his neck was badly burned. I cannot forget the bitter smell that lingered in the house even after an ambulance rushed Eric to the hospital.

A day or two before his accident, I had gotten into a conversation with Eric about the Emmaus story that was written on the wall over the couch he slept on. It seemed to him the rulers of Jerusalem, the people who had killed Jesus—the people from whom the two disciples were running away—were people like his father.

I agreed but then pointed out that Jesus didn't hate the people who played large or small parts in his crucifixion—he felt compassion for them. Dying on the cross he prayed for them to be forgiven. I asked if it could ever happen that he could see his father with compassion. What was behind his father's anger? Why was he so threatened by Eric's long hair? What in his formation had made it so hard for him to look at America's actions critically? What was driving his rage about his son who, like so many other young people at the time, opposed what America was doing in Vietnam?

During his days in the hospital, Eric explored these and other questions. Finally he gave me his home address and phone number and asked me to call his father. By the time Eric was ready to leave the hospital, his father was there to meet him and, with tears, asked Eric if they could make a new start. "No haircut needed, son." They left the hospital arm in arm.

If reconciliation between a parent and child can be hard, think how much harder it can be between those actively at war with each other. And yet it sometimes happens. Much depends on how the target of fear or anger responds.

During Christmas 1914, along the front lines of World War I, there was a brief glimpse of peace between enemies—an unauthorized truce involving roughly 100,000 British and German troops. A cessation of fighting occurred along the length of the Western Front when German troops began decorating the area around their trenches in the region of Ypres, Belgium, and Saint-Yvon. The Germans began by placing candles on their trenches and on Christmas trees, then continued their celebration by singing Christmas carols. The British responded with carols of their own. The two sides began shouting Christmas greetings to each other. Soon there were excursions across No Man's Land, where small gifts were exchanged— food, tobacco, and drink plus souvenirs such as buttons and hats. The artillery in the region fell silent. The truce also allowed a breathing spell during which recently killed soldiers could be brought back behind their lines by burial parties. Joint services were held. In many sectors, the truce lasted only through Christmas night, while in others it continued until New Year's Day.

One witness, Bruce Bairnsfather, wrote: "I wouldn't have missed that unique and weird Christmas Day for anything. . . . I spotted a German officer, some sort of lieutenant I should think, and being a bit of a collector, I intimated to him that I had taken a fancy to some of his buttons. . . . I brought out my wire clippers and, with a few deft snips, removed a couple of his buttons and put them in my pocket. I then gave him two of mine in exchange. . . . The last I saw was one of my machine gunners, who was a bit of an amateur hairdresser in civil life, cutting the unnaturally long hair of a docile Boche, who was patiently kneeling on the ground whilst the automatic clippers crept up the back of his neck."

The higher officers behind the lines were not pleased. Sir Horace Smith-Dorrien, commander of the British II Corps, issued orders forbidding friendly communication with the opposing German troops. Adolf Hitler, then a young corporal of the 16th Bavarian Reserve Infantry, was also an opponent of the truce.[1]

Compassion toward enemies occurred on a large scale in Moscow in the next-to-last year of the Second World War. Among the witnesses was the poet Yevgeny Yevtushenko, then still a child. He was standing at his mother's side on July 17, 1944, part of the crowd watching a procession of twenty thousand German war prisoners being marched across Red Square. Yevtushenko writes:

> *The pavements swarmed with onlookers, cordoned off by soldiers and police. The crowd was mostly women—Russian women with hands roughened by hard work, lips untouched by lipstick, and with thin hunched shoulders which had borne half of the burden of the war. Every one of them must have had a father or a husband, a brother or a son killed by the Germans. They gazed with hatred in the direction from which the column was to appear.*
>
> *At last we saw it. The generals marched at the head, massive chins stuck out, lips folded disdainfully, their whole demeanor meant to show superiority over their plebian victors. "They smell of perfume, the bastards," someone in the crowd said with hatred. The women were clenching their fists. The soldiers and policemen had all they could do to hold them back.*

---

1. See the Christmas truce entry in Wikipedia: http://en.wikipedia.org/wiki/Christmas_truce.

All at once something happened to them. They saw German soldiers, thin, unshaven, wearing dirty, blood-stained bandages, hobbling on crutches or leaning on the shoulders of their comrades; the soldiers walked with their heads down. The street became dead silent—the only sound was the shuffling of boots and the thumping of crutches.

Then I saw an elderly women in broken-down boots push herself forward and touch a policeman's shoulder, saying, "Let me through." There must have been something about her that made him step aside. She went up to the column, took from inside her coat something wrapped in a colored handkerchief and unfolded it. It was a crust of black bread. She pushed it awkwardly into the pocket of a soldier, so exhausted that he was tottering on his feet. And now from every side women were running toward the soldiers, pushing into their hands bread, cigarettes, whatever they had. The soldiers were no longer enemies. They were people.[2]

It was a truly eucharistic moment initiated by the compassion of one brave woman. Food was in short supply—everyone in the crowd was undernourished. Even the smallest scrap of bread was valuable. Yet hungry women gave bread to hungry enemies. We might say it was a reenactment of the miracle at Emmaus. Once again Christ was known in the breaking of bread.

2. Yevgeny Yevtushenko, *A Precocious Autobiography* (New York: Dutton, 1963), 26.

Battling Dragons, Taming Wolves, Befriending Lions

AMONG TRADITIONAL CHRISTIAN stories that challenge the Gospel according to John Wayne are tales of saints and beasts, the most well known of which is the legend of Saint George and the dragon.

If we search for the elusive figure of the historical Saint George, we quickly discover that he never saw a dragon nor did he rescue a princess in distress. It's even possible he was a farmer rather than a soldier—the name "George" means tiller of the soil; for this reason Saint George is a patron saint of agriculture, herds, flocks, and shepherds.

Saint George, born late in the third century, was one among many martyrs of the early church. What made him a saint especially loved and remembered was the fearless manner in which he proclaimed his faith during a period of fierce anti-Christian persecution initiated by the Emperor Diocletian in February 303. George was among the early victims. Over an eight-year period thousands were tortured and many executed while others were sent into exile as slave laborers in quarries and mines in Egypt and Palestine. Churches were destroyed and biblical texts burned. Most Christians did what they could to avoid being noticed.

According to one ancient account, far from concealing his faith, George went to a public square and announced, "All the gods of the pagans are devils. My God made the heavens and is the true God."[1] For this daring action Saint George was arrested, tortured,

---

1. For a succinct account both of the legend of Saint George and the historical person behind the legend, see the entry for the saint's feast day, April 23, in *Butler's Lives of the Saints,* ed. Herbert Thurston and Donald Attwater (New York: P. J. Kenedy, 1963).

and finally beheaded in the town of Nicomedia, in the northwest of modern Turkey. His body was brought to his birthplace, Diospolis, later known as Lydda and today as Lod in modern-day Israel. His witness led to the conversion of many and gave renewed courage to others already baptized.

In 311 the persecution ended. With Diocletian in retirement, the emperor Galerius (ill and close to death) published an edict of toleration allowing Christians to restore their places of worship and to worship in their own way without interference, provided they did nothing to disturb the peace.

A period of persecution ended, but the memory of those eight years of suffering would never be forgotten. George was one of the saints whose witness remained fresh and challenging. Icons of him were painted and hung in more and more churches. As centuries passed he became the patron saint of cities and whole countries.

In early icons, made long before a dragon became attached to his name, George was depicted as a soldier holding the cross of martyrdom. Perhaps he was in the army, but he may also have been shown in military clothing because he so perfectly exemplified the qualities that Saint Paul spoke of in his letter to the Ephesians in which he calls on Christ's followers to wear the helmet of salvation and the armor of righteousness, to be girded with truth, to clad their feet in the gospel of peace, to possess the sword of the Spirit which is the word of God, and to protect themselves from the devil's flaming arrows with the shield of faith (Ephesians 6:10-17). However, such symbolic use of a Roman soldier's equipment does not rule out the possibility that George was in fact a soldier. People from every class and profession were drawn to the gospel, soldiers among them. George may have been one of these.

It was only centuries later that the dragon legend emerged. The most widely circulated version is found in a medieval text, the *Legenda aurea* (the Golden Legend), a collection of saints' lives written by Blessed James de Voragine in about 1260. More than a thousand handwritten copies from the age before printed books have survived; it was a bestseller in its time. In the book's chapter on

George we meet a dragon that had been terrorizing the local people. In their fear they sacrificed their children, chosen by lot, to appease the creature's appetite and protect themselves. Finally it was the turn of the king's daughter, Elizabeth. As related in the text by Blessed James:

> *Then did the king array his daughter as if for her wedding and embraced and kissed her, gave her his blessing, and then led her to the place where the dragon was.*
>
> *When she was there Saint George passed by, and when he saw the lady asked what brought her to this place. She replied, "Go your way, fair young man, so that you will not perish also."*
>
> *Then said he, "Tell me what the matter is, why you weep, and fear nothing."*
>
> *When she saw that he insisted on knowing, she said to him how she was delivered to the dragon. Then Saint George said, "Fair daughter, have no fear for I will help you in the name of Jesus Christ."*
>
> *She responded, "For God's sake, good knight, go your way and leave me here, for you cannot rescue me."*
>
> *While they were talking, the dragon appeared and came rushing toward them. Saint George was upon his horse. Making the sign of the cross, he rode bravely against the dragon and struck him with his spear, wounding him badly and throwing him to the ground.*
>
> *Then he said to the maid, "Take your belt and bind it about the neck of the dragon and be not afraid."*
>
> *When she had done so the dragon followed her as if it were a meek beast and debonair, leading him into the city.*[2]

The legend ends with George calling on the local people to be baptized. The king agrees, also promising to build and maintain churches, honor the clergy, faithfully attend religious services, and be generous to the poor.

From the point of view of history, the story is pure myth. Yet

---

2. For the full text of the George narrative as told in the *Legenda aurea*, see http://www.aug.edu/augusta/iconography/goldenLegend/george.htm.

when you think about it, what better way to symbolize the evil that George actually confronted and defeated—the ruthless power of an emperor—than to portray it in the form of a fire-breathing dragon? George fought and, in embracing martyrdom, was victorious over a dragon-like adversary whose methods terrified and silenced most people at the time. We can understand the dragon as representing anything that makes us afraid and leads us to conform to a death-dealing society.

The white horse George rides in icons and paintings, a graceful creature as light as air and as fearless as his rider, represents the courage God gave to George in his disobedience to the emperor. It is the courage God gives to any Christian who would prefer to die rather than to collaborate with evil.

In many versions of the Saint George icon, the lance the hero holds is shown resting lightly in his open hand, meaning that it is the power of God rather than the strength of man that overcomes evil. The lance is usually shown as being pencil thin and often has a small cross at the top, thus stressing visually that it is not with weapons of war that evil is overcome but with the power of the life-giving cross—the cross that opens the path to the Resurrection. Similarly, even in his battle with the dragon, George's face shows not a trace of anger, hatred, or anxiety. His tranquil face serves to remind the viewer of Christ's commandment that his followers must love their enemies even in resisting them.

In more detailed versions of the icon there are scenes from before and after the battle with the dragon. Sometimes a castle is in the background from which Elizabeth's parents watch all that happens. Icons sometimes show Elizabeth leading the defeated dragon on a leash made of her belt, the enemy made tame—a symbol of victory of life over death similar to Christ's Resurrection.

Bringing a wounded but still living dragon back to the town provides us with a powerful image of transformation. The final fruit of George's combat with the dragon is not victory over a monster or financial reward for successful combat but the inspiration George gave to unbelieving people to embrace conversion. The time of worshipping dragons and sacrificing one's children to them is over.

True stories become streamlined into legends, and legends become compressed into myths, as the tale of Saint George bears witness, but there are many stories of the encounters of saints with beasts that may stand on more solid historical foundations.

One of them concerns one of the greatest medieval saints, Francis of Assisi.[3] Toward the end of his life he received an appeal for help from the people of Gubbio, an ancient Umbrian walled town north of Assisi. Their problem was a huge wolf that attacked not only animals but people, so that the men had to arm themselves as if for combat before going outside the town walls. They felt as if Gubbio were under siege.

What the townspeople expected of Francis is not clear, but when Francis said he intended to meet the wolf face-to-face, they sought to dissuade him. They had no desire to cause the death of a neighbor who had long since sworn off the possession or use of any weapon. What chance could an unarmed man wearing a cloak of rags have against a wild animal? But according to the *Fioretti*, the principal collection of stories of the saint's life,

> *Francis placed his hope in the Lord Jesus Christ, master of all creatures. Protected neither by shield or helmet, only arming himself with the sign of the Cross, he bravely set out of the town with his companion, putting his faith in the Lord who makes those who*

---

3. Thanks to Saint Francis of Assisi, there was a period in the thirteenth century when many Christians in the West refused to take part in war and were, remarkably, even given papal support. Francis founded a society for lay people, a "third order," whose rule called on members to be unarmed peacemakers: "They are to be reconciled with their neighbors and [are] to restore what belongs to others. . . . They are not to take up deadly weapons, or bear them about, against anybody. . . . They are to refrain from formal oaths [which might bind them to military service]. . . . They are to perform the works of mercy: visiting and caring for the sick, burying the dead, and caring for the poor. . . . They should seek the reconciliation of enemies, both among their members and among non-members." See Arnaldo Fortini, *Francis of Assisi* (New York: Crossroad, 1981), 522; also for an outline of the rule and its history, see http://en.wikipedia.org/wiki/Third_Order_of_Saint_Francis.

> *believe in him walk without injury on an asp . . . and trample not*
> *merely on a wolf but even a lion and a dragon.*

While keeping a safe distance, some local peasants followed Francis. Finally the wolf saw Francis and came running as if to attack. The story continues,

> *The saint made the sign of the Cross, and the power of God . . .*
> *stopped the wolf, making it slow down and close its cruel mouth.*
> *Then Francis called to it, "Brother Wolf, in the name of Jesus Christ,*
> *I order you not to hurt me or anyone."*

The wolf came up to Francis, lowered his head, and then lay down at his feet as though he were a pet dog. Francis then censured the wolf for its former cruelties, especially for killing human beings made in the image of God, thus making a whole town into his deadly enemy. Francis said,

> *"But, Brother Wolf, I want to make peace between you and them,*
> *so that they will not be harmed by you any more, and after they*
> *have forgiven you your past crimes, neither men nor dogs will pur-*
> *sue you anymore."*

The wolf responded with gestures of submission, "showing that it willingly accepted what the saint had said and would observe it."

Francis promised the wolf that the people of Gubbio would henceforth "give you food every day as long as you shall live, so that you will never again suffer hunger." In return, the wolf had to give up attacking both animal and man. "And as Saint Francis held out his hand to receive the pledge, the wolf also raised its front paw and meekly and gently put it in Saint Francis's hand as a sign that it had given its pledge."

Francis led the wolf back into Gubbio, where the nervous local populace met them in the market square. Here Francis preached a sermon in which he said "calamities were permitted by God because of our sins and that the fires of hell are far worse than the jaws of a wolf which can only kill the body." He called on the people to do penance in order to be "free from the wolf in this world and from the devouring fire of hell in the next world." Pledging himself as "bonds-man for Brother Wolf," Francis assured them that the wolf would now live in peace with them, but that they were now obliged to feed him every day.

After living harmlessly within the walls of Gubbio for two years, "the wolf grew old and died, and the people were sorry, because whenever it went through the town, its peaceful kindness and patience reminded them of the virtues and holiness of Saint Francis."

Is the story true in the journalistic sense? Or is the wolf a story-teller's metaphor for the effect Francis often had on violent, wolf-like men? While the story works on both levels, there is reason to believe there was indeed a wolf of Gubbio. A Franciscan friend of ours, Sister Rosemary Lynch, told me that, during restoration work, the bones of a wolf were found buried within a church in Gubbio.

Another saint remembered for peaceful relations with wild ani-mals is Gerasimos of the Jordan, shown in icons holding the paw of a lion. The story behind the image comes down to us from Saint John Moschos, a monk of Saint Theodosius Monastery near Bethlehem and author of *The Spiritual Meadow*, a book written in the course of journeys he made in the late sixth century. It's a collection of stories of monastic saints, mainly desert dwellers, and also can be regarded as a very early example of travel writing.

In the fifth century Gerasimos was abbot of a community of seventy monks who lived in the desert east of Jericho, a mile from the River Jordan. The monks slept on reed mats, had cells with-out doors, and—apart from common prayer—normally observed silence. Their diet consisted chiefly of water, dates, and bread. Gerasimos, in ongoing repentance for having been influenced by the teachings of a heretic in his youth, is said to have eaten even less than the norm.

One day, while walking along the Jordan, Gerasimos came upon a lion roaring in agony because of a large splinter imbedded in one paw. Overcome with compassion for the suffering beast, Gerasimos removed the splinter, drained and cleaned the wound, then bound it up, expecting the lion would return to its cave. Instead, the creature meekly followed him back to the monastery and became the abbot's devoted pet. The whole community was amazed at the lion's apparent conversion to a peaceful life—he now lived on bread and vegetables—and its devotion to the abbot.

The lion was given the special task of guarding the community's donkey, which was pastured along the Jordan. But one day it happened that, while the lion napped, the donkey was stolen by a passing trader. After searching without success, the lion returned to the monastery, its head hanging low. The brothers concluded the lion had been overcome by its instinctual appetite for meat. As punishment the lion was given the donkey's job of carrying water each day from the river to the monastery in a saddle pack fitted with four earthen jars.

A year later, it happened that the same trader was coming along the Jordan with the stolen donkey and three camels. The lion recognized the donkey and roared so loudly that the trader ran away. Taking its rope in his jaws, the lion led the donkey back to the monastery with the camels following behind. The monks realized, to their shame, that they had misjudged the lion. The same day Gerasimos gave the lion a name: Jordanes. The repentant trader afterward delivered an annual gift of olive oil to the monastery.

For five more years, until the abbot's death, Jordanes was part of the monastic community. When the elder fell asleep in the Lord and was buried, Jordanes lay down on the grave, roaring its grief and beating its head against the ground. Finally Jordanes rolled over and died on the last resting place of Gerasimos.

The narrative touches the reader intimately, inspiring the hope that the wild beast that still roars within us may yet be pacified, while the story's second half suggests that, when falsely accused of having returned to an unconverted life, vindication may finally happen.

The icon of Saint Gerasimos focuses on a moment of physical contact between monk and lion—an Eden-like moment with an act of healing at its core. By the river of Christ's baptism, the Jordan, an ancient harmony we associate with Adam and Eve before the Fall is renewed. Enmity is over between humanity and creation, at least for a time in the small island of peace brought into being through one man's merciful action. The icon presents us with an image of peace—human and beast no longer threatening each other's life.

But again the question arises: Is the story true? Certainly Abbot Gerasimos is real. Many texts refer to him. He was one of the participants in the Fourth Ecumenical Council at Chalcedon in AD 451. Soon after his death he was recognized as a saint. The monastery he founded lasted for centuries, a center of spiritual life and a place of pilgrimage. He is remembered as one of the great elders of the desert. But what about Jordanes? Might the lion be just a graphic metaphor for Gerasimos's ability to convert some of the lion-like people who came to him? Or might the story be as real as any event in today's news reports?

Unlikely stories about saints are not rare. Some are so remarkable—for example, the legend of Saint Nicholas bringing back to life three murdered children whose bodies had been hacked to pieces and then boiled in a stew pot—that the miracles related in the four Gospels seem not so impressive by comparison. Yet even the most farfetched legend usually has a basis in the character of the saint: Nicholas was tireless and resourceful in his efforts to protect the lives of the defenseless. On one occasion he prevented the execution of three young men who had been condemned to death. In icons that include biographical scenes, we find him grasping an executioner's blade that was about to fall on one prisoner's neck. It's a story that has the ring of truth in the most prosaic sense. The miracle here is the saint's courage in saving lives while endangering his own. Christ's mercy shines through Nicholas's act of intervention.

A Gerasimos-like story comes down to us from the life of Saint Seraphim of Sarov, one of the towering figures of eighteenth-century Russia. In some icons he is shown feeding a bear at the door of his log cabin. Living deep in the Russian forest, visitors occasionally found Seraphim sharing his ration of bread with bears and wolves. "How is it," he was asked, "that you have enough bread in your bag for all of them?" "There is always enough," Seraphim answered. He once remarked of a bear that visited him, "I understand fasting, but he does not."

It's not unlikely that Jordanes was as real as Seraphim's bear. In the fifth century, lions could still be found in the wilderness along the Jordan. We can easily imagine Gerasimos as a man from whom all fear had been burned away by compassion.

Lions have a special place in the human imagination. From the classical world to our own era, the lion has chiefly been regarded as danger incarnate, the most iconic image of "nature red in tooth and claw." And yet at times the symbol is transfigured. The lion becomes an image of beauty, grace, and courage. In *The Narnia Chronicles*, C. S. Lewis chose a lion to represent Christ. The handsome stone lions on guard outside the main entrance of the New York Public Library have always struck me as guardians of truth and wisdom.

There is still one more wrinkle to the ancient story of Gerasimos and Jordanes. Saint Jerome, the great scholar responsible for rendering the Bible from Hebrew and Greek into Latin, long honored in the West as patron saint of translators, lived for years in a cave near the place of Christ's Nativity in Bethlehem, only a two-day walk from Gerasimos's monastery. The name of Gerasimos is not very different from Geronimus, the Latin word for Jerome. Pilgrims from the West apparently connected the story told of Gerasimos with Jerome. Given the fact that Jerome sometimes wrote letters with a lionish bite, perhaps it's appropriate that Gerasimos's lion eventually wandered into images of Jerome. It's rare to find a painting of Jerome in which the lion is absent.[4]

The stories of the man-and-beast encounters of Francis of Assisi, Gerasimos of the Jordan, and Seraphim of Sarov are parables of the conversion of enmity into friendship. For the would-be peacemaker, it wouldn't be a bad idea to have an icon of at least one of these saints somewhere in your home. Need an image to stimulate courage? Get an icon of Saint George battling the dragon.

---

4. For those who want a bigger helping of such stories than this chapter provides, I recommend *Beasts and Saints,* trans. Helen Waddell; woodcuts by Robert Gibbings (New York: H. Holt, 1934). The copy in our house, appropriately, has teeth marks in it from a dog that wanted to show her appreciation.

Graced Moments

MAKING FRIENDS OF ENEMIES—and making choices not driven by enmity—happens thanks not only to an inner act of will but still more to the grace we receive from the Holy Spirit. The word *grace* is often used to describe the transformed state of being that occurs at moments when God enters into our conscious lives. While the obstacles within ourselves often seem impossible to overcome— deeply entrenched boredom, indifference, prejudice, anger, and hatred—the wind of grace can suddenly blow away walls that seemed immoveable and impenetrable. We can speak of "graced moments" when we see another person in such a light that we realize that, until that moment, we were blind. We "saw," but in so superficial and limited a way that we were unaware of God's presence in that other life. The other was more a thing than a person.

Invariably those graced occasions when God breaks through in us are turning points. We are changed and, even if held captive within the stone walls of a prison, we experience a deep freedom and unspeakable happiness. For the rest of our lives we know that what the French writer Leon Bloy said is true: "Joy is the most infallible sign of the presence of God."

During a semester when I was teaching a first-year theology course at the College of New Rochelle, not far from New York City, I quickly became aware that we needed to focus on very basic questions. Though nearly all the students had gone to Catholic high schools, they had now reached the age of doubt. Most of them questioned the existence of God, at least a God who might take an interest in them personally, a God who knows each person by name. I responded by writing Bloy's sentence about joy on the blackboard and then asked each student to write a paper in the coming week on some personal experience of joy that might in fact have been, though

Icon of the Transfiguration

unrecognized at the time, a meeting in the darkness with God. I pointed out that God does not enter our lives wearing a badge that says "Hello, my name is God." God meets us namelessly, silently, unrecognized, and by surprise, beyond expectations and outside all boxes. Such meetings can happen not only in churches but in zoos, supermarkets, and subways.

Mystical encounters, I suggested, are not uncommon; only it doesn't occur to us to call them that. Afterward we often marginalize their significance, putting them in a section of memory where we store puzzles and mysteries, all the bits that stand outside everyday life and all usual categories. What would happen to us if we explored them more actively, seeing in them clues to who we are and what God is calling us to do with our lives?

The papers I received were deeply moving. I learned long afterward that for some students the papers they wrote on graced moments in their lives were turning points along the way to an adult faith.

My wife, Nancy, provides an example of such an experience. It occurred when she was a sixteen-year-old high school student. It's an event she sometimes refers to as "my vision at the bus stop." She explains:

I call it a vision because I truly believe that God sent it to me for a reason; that it was some supernatural interference intended to add something to my thought pool. It happened on a warm, beautiful spring afternoon. I was coming home from high school, the last lone student on the school bus. I stepped off the bus at my stop, a street corner in an altogether ordinary suburban New Jersey setting, and as the bus pulled away I felt something strange. It was as though I could feel the world as a globe, and I could feel it turning around. I sensed that I was a figure on that globe. I stood still and felt the steady move-ment of the world, around and around. It was as though I were at the uppermost point, a sort of pole, and the world was turning around on the axis on which I stood. It was such a real feeling that I had to steady myself to keep from falling over. Then I slowly turned around on my axis and gazed at what was visible from where I stood: the four houses on the four corners of the crossroad, the tall pine trees in all the front yards, the mailboxes. And I realized that there was nobody in the whole world who could see what I was seeing from my great height: not even famous people, not even the president or the Beatles, not even terribly rich people. It wasn't that my view was so special, but I suddenly knew that it was entirely unique.

I remember going home and telling my mother, "Mom, I just felt like I was my own North Pole!" I could understand the vision no further than that at the time. But it has remained a fountain of understanding for me. The older I grew the more it revealed to me about myself, about other people, about God. I can say that this vision is the most important thing that happened to me in my life, and I am certain that it was a gift from God who could see that I needed something very big very fast.

In time I might have dismissed the vision as simply odd and ado-lescent, but I began reading about other people who have had the same experience. It's been like finding out that other people have dreams about missing final exams, when you thought you were the only one.

Years later, during a three-month sabbatical period when Nancy and I were living at the Ecumenical Institute mid-way between Jerusalem and Bethlehem, Nancy's childhood experience was repeated at the top of Mount Tabor, the site of the Transfiguration, half-way between Nazareth and the Sea of Galilee. Here she describes what happened:

> *We drove up the steep, narrow road to the church at the top of the mountain, parked our rented car, and went inside. Like so many of the churches built on the holy sites, this one was breathtaking in its dimensions and decoration. But one interesting aspect of this particular church caught my attention: a round circle laid in the stonework floor in the center of the church, with an X transecting it. I went up to this circle and stood in the center of the X, and suddenly it happened again: the polar vision, the unmistakable brush with pure reality. Only this time I found myself standing not on my New Jersey bus stop but on the Pole of Poles: the place where the Lord himself had been transfigured before his disciples. Of course, the X had been laid in the floor to indicate the place of the Transfiguration. But when I stood there myself and the whole earth fell away from me on all sides, I was able to draw some unavoidable conclusions: that . . . the very center of the human individual is God, and that we are so confused and distracted by sin that we are almost never able to be there, where we should be, where we are truly ourselves, where God is. If that were possible, we would be transfigured, too. We would shine like the sun.*[1]

I think too of various graced moments Thomas Merton described in his autobiography, *The Seven Storey Mountain*, in which he chronicles his conversion to Christianity. There was an overwhelming experience of God's reality and presence when, as an eighteen-year-old tourist in Rome, after days of being bored and irritated by many of the major guidebook sites, he found himself drawn to the city's most ancient churches in which much of the mosaic art of Christianity's first millennium was still to be seen. "I was fascinated by these Byzantine mosaics. I began to haunt the churches where they

---

1. Nancy Forest, "Right Where I'm Standing," www.jimandnancyforest.com/2010/01/20/right-where-im-standing/.

were to be found. . . . Without knowing anything about it, I became a pilgrim."[2]

The icons that so arrested Merton were windows through which he felt Christ's gaze. The experience was his first glimpse of a life rooted in Christianity. As he wrote in *The Seven Storey Mountain*,

> For the first time in my whole life I began to find out something of who this Person was that men call Christ. It was obscure, but it was a true knowledge of Him. But it was in Rome that my conception of Christ was formed. It was there I first saw Him, Whom I now serve as my God and my King, and who owns and rules my life. It is the Christ of the Apocalypse, the Christ of the Martyrs, the Christ of the Fathers. It is the Christ of Saint John, and of Saint Paul, and of Saint Augustine and Saint Jerome and all the Fathers, and the Desert Fathers. It is Christ God, Christ King.[3]

After a complex journey with many detours, Merton was eventually received into the Catholic Church and several years later entered monastic life. He had been a monk for nearly twenty years when another turning point in his life occurred, an intense experience of God's presence in others and God's love for them—people whom Merton might otherwise have regarded as unknowable strangers. It happened when he had occasion to be in Louisville, the city closest to his monastery, waiting at a busy downtown intersection for the crossing light to change. Here is what he had to say about what happened:

> In Louisville, at the corner of Fourth and Walnut, in the center of the shopping district, I was suddenly overwhelmed by the realization that I loved all those people, that they were mine and I theirs, that we could not be alien to one another even though we were total strangers. It was like waking from a dream of separateness, of spurious self-isolation in a special world, the world of renunciation

2. Thomas Merton, *The Seven Storey Mountain* (New York: Harcourt Brace, 1947), 108.

3. Ibid., 108-9.

A sign at the corner of Fourth and Walnut in Louisville

and supposed holiness. The whole illusion of a separate holy existence is a dream. . . . This sense of liberation from an illusory difference was such a relief and such a joy to me that I almost laughed out loud. . . . It is a glorious destiny to be a member of the human race, though it is a race dedicated to many absurdities and one which makes many terrible mistakes: yet, with all that, God Himself gloried in becoming a member of the human race. A member of the human race! To think that such a commonplace realization should suddenly seem like news that one holds the winning ticket in a cosmic sweepstake. . . .There is no way of telling people that they are all walking around shining like the sun. . . . There are no strangers. . . . If only we could see each other [as we really are] all the time. There would be no more war, no more hatred, no more cruelty, no more greed. . . . I suppose the big problem is that we would fall down and worship each other. . . . [T]he gate of heaven is everywhere.[4]

At the most unlikely time and place, waiting for a red light to turn green, Merton had an eye-opening experience of a truth that normally seems hard to believe: that each of us really does bear the image of God. It isn't a fable or wishful thinking but as real as the ground we're standing on. However damaged people have been by all that has happened in their lives and the destructive choices they've made, the spark of the divine has not been and cannot be completely snuffed out. In a moment of grace, Merton saw the strangers around

---

4. Merton, *Conjectures*, 140-42.

him as if with God's eyes and experienced God's measureless love for each of us.

Each graced moment has its special impact. The one in Louisville helped Merton to see himself and his monastic vocation in a new light. He realized that a religious community, however geographically isolated, is not and cannot be an "escape from the world" but rather a place of deep engagement "in the struggles and sufferings of the world."[5] In his correspondence and writings he began to put special stress on issues relating to war and peace and on the qualities a would-be peacemaker needs to cultivate, starting with compassion.

What happened to Merton while standing at Fourth and Walnut—an intersection since renamed Thomas Merton Square—is expressed in a different way in a Jewish story in which a rabbi asks his students, "When can we know that the night has ended and the day begun?" "Is it the moment," one student proposes, "when you can tell the difference between a sheep and a dog?" "No," said the rabbi. "Is it," asks another student, "when you can see the difference between a fig tree and an olive tree?" "Not that either." The students ask in one voice, "Then when is it?" The rabbi answers, "It is the moment when you can look at a face never seen before and recognize the stranger as a brother or sister. Until that moment, no matter how bright the day, it is still the night."

Most of us would have to admit that we are living mainly in the night. Instead of seeing sisters and brothers, we tend to see labels: white or black, male or female, straight or gay, liberal or conservative, rich or poor, friend or enemy. We come to know whom to welcome and whom to keep at a distance, whom to care for and whom to ignore. We become committed citizens of the night.

---

5. Thomas Merton, *Honorable Reader: Reflections on My Work* (New York: Crossroad, 1989), 63-67.

Fear in the Dark

> *I sought the Lord and he answered me*
> *and delivered me from all my fears.*
> — Psalm 34:4

DAWN AT MIDNIGHT. God appearing when least expected. Heaven revealing itself at the most unlikely place and to the most unlikely people. Consider this account of daybreak occurring in the middle of the night in the countryside east of Bethlehem:

> *And in that region there were shepherds out in the field, keeping watch over their flock by night. And an angel of the Lord appeared to them, and the glory of the Lord shone around them, and they were filled with fear. And the angel said to them, "Be not afraid."* (Luke 2:8-10)

A key word in the Nativity narrative is fear. What the shepherds saw and heard was frightening. Whatever angels look like when they make themselves visible, they are not winged dolls. The Gospel author Luke writes about fear in the night and the angelic summons to set fear aside.

No doubt fear had long been a familiar dimension of the shepherds' lives. Not only were they, as shepherds, men living on society's margins, but there were good grounds for dread in their day-to-day world. There were the Roman occupiers, and there was also King Herod. No one familiar with Herod's ways would be surprised that his response to the messianic birth was to order the slaughter of all the youngest sons of Bethlehem.

There are two very different sorts of fear that figure in biblical texts: fear of other people and fear of God. Paradoxically, it is fear of God—a state of awe reflecting our consciousness of the power and majesty of God as creator and ruler of the universe coupled with the awareness of God holding us accountable for what we do and fail to do with our lives and talents—that raises up the most fearless people. The unholy fear we are called away from both by angels and by Jesus is that fear which inspires cowardice, makes us deaf to conscience, blocks us from responding to those around us, makes us insensitive to others, blinds us

Byzantine Nativity bas relief

in such a way that we fail to recognize others, including our enemies, as brothers and sisters.

"Be not afraid," said the angels. Fear is the wall that keeps us far from both God and our neighbor. As the Orthodox theologian Metropolitan John Zizioulas has written,

> *The essence of sin is the fear of the Other, which is part of the rejection of God. Once the affirmation of the "self" is realized through the rejection and not the acceptance of the Other . . . it is only natural and inevitable for the other to become an enemy and a threat. Reconciliation with God is a necessary pre-condition for reconciliation with any "other."*

It's equally true to say that reconciliation with one's neighbor is a necessary precondition for reconciliation with God.

Zizioulas continues:

> *The fact that the fear of the other is pathologically inherent in our existence results in the fear not only of the other but of all otherness. This is a delicate point requiring careful consideration, for it shows how deep and widespread fear of the other is: we are not afraid simply of certain others, but even if we accept them, it is on*

condition that they are somehow like ourselves. Radical otherness is an anathema. Difference itself is a threat. That this is universal and pathological is to be seen in the fact that even when difference does not in actual fact constitute a threat for us, we reject it simply because we dislike it. Again and again we notice that fear of the other is nothing more than fear of the different. We all want somehow to project into the other the model of our own selves.[1]

It is fear that contaminates our spiritual life and, at the same time, our public life. Because of fear, we take care to avoid anyone who might be dangerous—the "anyone" becoming not just particular individuals but huge smudged categories of human beings who raise our alarm flags by their differences: their skin color, accent, clothing, neighborhood, religion, or nationality.

The point isn't that there is nothing to fear—there's plenty to fear—but that the self-protective cage we create and inhabit, supposedly a safe place, is in reality a cramped and miserable place to live in, and scary in its own right.

Christian faith isn't an escape from the real world and its terrors—quite the opposite. What we see through the lens of habitual fear isn't reality but a wildly distorted carnival mirror. The lens of fear is recreated and reshaped daily by news reports that focus on crime, violence, war, acts of terrorism, child abuse, and other assaults on human decency. "If it bleeds it leads" is a journalistic proverb I learned as a young reporter. Bloodshed is automatically page-one news while actions that prevent violence or save life tend to get short shrift on the inside pages or are used as "human interest" stories, if space permits. The violence that makes headlines is real and cannot be ignored, but to over-report and over-consume such news gradually deforms our perception of who we are and what it means to be human. The realism we need involves an integration of perception that takes account both of the grim *and* the life sustaining. In the process we discover that, while murderers exist, vastly more of us

---

1. From a lecture given at the European Orthodox Congress in October 1993. The text is online: www.incommunion.org/2012/07/23/communion-and-otherness-2/.

are involved in caring for life rather than destroying it. Violence is not our default setting.

Nicholas Berdyaev was a philosopher who, in the early days of the Russian revolution, was a Marxist but later became one of the most compelling Christian voices of the twentieth century. He took away from his engagement with Marxism a commitment to see things as they are, whether hellish or heavenly. Rose-colored glasses were not allowed. As he wrote,

> It is the Christian duty to look reality in the face and to keep ourselves fully conscious of it. Nothing is more unchristian than the "idealization" of reality; it is precisely the Christian more than anybody else who must put aside fear whenever the exposure and condemnation of a horrible and wicked reality is called for. . . . The human body must be seen naked to know its beauty, and in the same way Christianity demands that realities be stripped of their artificial adornments.[2]

Thomas Merton had much in common with Berdyaev, including the constant struggle to see reality free of illusion—in Christian terms, to be aware of both the crucifixion and the Resurrection. During the last decade of his life, Merton became more and more engaged in reflection on war and social disorder and attentive to the role fear plays in both our political and our spiritual lives. "The root of war is fear," he argued in one of his essays. It is "not so much the fear men have of one another as the fear they have of everything. It is not that they do not trust one another, they do not even trust themselves." Out of our fear, Merton argued, the human race has taken itself to the edge of self-extinction. An authentic Christianity, Merton wrote, must shake off fear and every notion of an incinerator god and instead commit itself "to the total abolition of war" much as earlier Christians struggled for the abolition of slavery.[3]

I was on the *Catholic Worker* staff when Merton's essay was published and sent a copy of that issue to my father, a Marxist. "It's good as far as it goes," my father wrote in his reply, "and it's certainly encour-

---

2. Nicholas Berdyaev, *Christianity and Class War* (London: Sheed & Ward, 1933).

3. *The Catholic Worker*, October 1961.

aging to see a Catholic writer of such prominence thinking critically about war, but I have to disagree with the central thesis. As I see it, the root of war is bad economics." It was a thoughtful response—bad economics is indeed a major factor behind war. However our exchange didn't end there. Several years later he wrote me to say, "I keep thinking of what Merton wrote and just want you to know that I have come to realize that the root of bad economics is fear."

It's helpful to look at Jesus' life with special attention to the theme of fear. In the years he undertakes his public ministry, we see him abandoning the securities of normal life to become a homeless person, a refugee in his own homeland, a wandering teacher. "The foxes have their holes and the birds their nests," he remarked, "but the son of man has nowhere to lay his head" (Matthew 8:20).

The Gospels provide many examples of Jesus overcoming fear. He has the courage to be with, even to be touched by, people in a legal condition (according the Mosaic law) of "uncleanness": lepers, bleeding women, the dead. He associates with despised or marginalized people—prostitutes, tax collectors, Samaritans, Roman soldiers. We see in such associations that he has overcome one of the strongest dreads, the fear of condemnation and rejection by one's peers. He had the courage to turn over the money tables in the Temple. He was without fear in his encounters with those who arrested him, judged him, tortured him, and crucified him. His disciples, on the other hand, were often constrained by fear, with all but a few brave women and only one man, the disciple John, present for the crucifixion.

"Be not afraid": these few words are at the heart of the gospel. Trapped in fear, we are powerless to become disciples. As a result there is very little we can do about the double commandment: to love God and to love one another.

Jesus is the great joy announced by the angels to the shepherds precisely because he shows us that we do not have to center our lives on fear, fear of enemies or of all the other terrors life holds for us, even fear of death. In offering us an example of a life lived without fear, Jesus liberates us from being imprisoned in fear; not that we will never experience fear, but that fear will no longer take the place of God in our lives. Fear will no longer be the mainspring.

Enemies at One's Table

"IT'S QUITE EASY to say wonderful things about love, especially between wars," a retired British general once said to me during a break in a conference we were both attending in England. "It's like being a vegetarian between meals. But what about World War II? You weren't even wearing your first nappies when people like me were faced with the Nazis and bombs were falling on our houses. What would you have had us do? Drop Bibles on Germany?"

Not long after, at a meeting in Kiev in what was then still the Soviet Union, I met a Ukrainian Jew. "I am the sole survivor in my family," he said in halting English. "The only one. My parents, my grandparents, my sisters, my brothers, my cousins—all dead. You cannot imagine what the Nazis did. What could anyone do but fight back? What would you have done?"

In both cases I could only say I don't know what I would have done. World War II was already being fought when I was born—I wasn't yet four when it ended. Had I been old enough, I might well have been a soldier, even a volunteer, but I was too young to know exactly what war meant; for me it mainly meant that my father was far away, a soldier on an island somewhere in the Pacific Ocean.

How can one regard those who risked and often lost their lives fighting under arms against various forms of fascism except with respect and admiration? Yet I think often, with astonishment, of those who resisted Nazism without taking up weapons and wonder if I would have had the courage to be one of them.

In any event the question that faces us, rather than our parents and grandparents, is not what we would have done at some earlier time, nor is it to blame anyone who finds no method of defense of one's nation except through violence. The question is what can we do, now and in the future, to prevent war and bring to an end those wars now going on?

Still, it can be helpful to consider World War II and become aware that there were many people who used nonviolent methods in their struggle against the Nazis. Perhaps their example and courage may give us clues about alternatives to war in the future.

One of Hitler's unarmed opponents was Kasper Mayr, a secretary of the International Fellowship of Reconciliation, an ecumenical movement that promotes nonviolent approaches to conflict resolution and overcoming injustice. Though I never met Kasper Mayr, his daughter, Hildegard Goss-Mayr, is an old friend and long-time co-worker. She and her husband, Jean, have many times been nominated for the Nobel Peace Prize for their work in Europe, Latin America, the Pacific, and Asia.

As a twelve-year-old child, Hildegard was among the crowds of school children greeting Hitler when he entered Vienna following Austria's annexation to Germany in March 1938. As Hildegard told me,

> *The convoy of cars appeared and there was Hitler standing in one of them. Everyone around me was lifting their hands and shouting, "Heil Hitler! Heil Hitler!" It was the first time that I felt that there really is a strength of evil, something that is stronger than any individual being. I experienced the fascination that came from Hitler, that manipulation of masses of people. Evil can have a tremendous attraction. Thanks to what I learned at home I was determined not to lift my hand or to join in the shouting. I thought, "Even if they kill me, I am not going to lift up my hand." It was extremely hard.*

Only by holding her right wrist with her left hand was she able to restrain the impulse to act in unity with the crowd. The struggle was so intense that afterward she found that her grip had caused bruises.

The Mayr home, with its large garden and fruit trees, still stands on the outskirts of Vienna. As Russian troops closed in on what had been one of the principal cities of the Third Reich, the citizens of Vienna—even those few, like Kasper Mayr, who had resisted the Nazis—had every reason for dread. Hitler's armies, to which many thousands of Austrian men had belonged, had caused at least twenty million deaths in Soviet Russia, while destroying industrial centers and leaving many cities in ruins.

"Here was a victorious army," Hildegard recalls, "that would take revenge, that would rape its way to the center of the city. In the face of these expectations, my father had closed the door to our house but did not lock it." With his wife, daughter, and some family guests in the cellar, he waited upstairs, no doubt in prayer.

> *When the Russians approached and pounded against the door with their guns, father opened it and stood before them in a way they could not have expected. He pushed aside their rifles and gestured that they should come in, as if they were invited guests. Of course a soldier's attitude at such a moment is one of suspicion. He has seen six years of war and wants to survive. He is ready to shoot before he is shot. But they saw in my father's gesture that perhaps their fear was not necessary. They looked in the house to see if it was a trap. They found it wasn't. My father could see that they were relieved. They took off their rifles. And then my father called the others up from the basement. He was able to create an atmosphere of welcome, of trust, of love, of belonging.*

Far from raping the women and killing any of the occupants of the house, the soldiers were moved to share their own meager rations. "They could see how thin and hungry we were—for the city had been cut off for quite some time. They shared with our family and guests from their own food. Noticing a Russian icon on our living room wall, a soldier crossed himself and prayed in front of it. Others joined him."

It was one of those moments when, for those who live by the Gospel according to John Wayne, one relies on locked doors and guns rather than gestures of welcome. But as Hildegard points out,

> *If father had used a weapon, he could not have protected those others in the house, who might have been raped and even killed. If my father had been armed, the Russian soldiers would have been confirmed in their fears. Instead, out of his inner strength and calm,*

he was able to affirm their humanity and to take them out of the terrible way of war. Nobody is an angel, and war often brings out the worst in people. My father's approach made it more likely to bring out the best, but of course you never know what will happen. Those soldiers might have acted violently no matter what my father did. Still, when you believe in the strength of truth and love, you must respond this way no matter what the danger is. You have to prefer to be killed yourself rather than to kill another.[1]

Yes, you might say, there are moments when the highly motivated individual manages to do something remarkable. But these are exceptional people—heroes and saints, not ordinary people.

But consider another story from the Hitler years. Le Chambon-sur-Lignon is a town in the mountains of southern France. Here seven hundred townspeople plus two thousand peasants on outlying farms together managed to save thousands of Jews from the Holocaust. Inspired by a phrase found in the book of Numbers,[2] they made Le Chambon "a city of refuge"—a place of sanctuary and assistance for those in danger. The town's Protestant pastor, André Trocmé, and his wife, Magda, called on their neighbors not to "give up their consciences by assisting in the hatred, betrayal, and murder" of the collaborating French state and the Nazi occupiers but to instead offer hospitality and assistance to fleeing Jews. It is estimated that between 1942 and 1945, roughly 3,500 Jews were fed, housed, supplied with false papers, and, through a network of partners, smuggled to safety across the border into Switzerland.

The villagers' peaceful resistance was grounded on two unshakeable principles that Trocmé returned to again and again in his Sunday sermons. The first was that a Christian's first loyalty is to God

---

1. Interview with the author.

2. Numbers 35:9-12: "Then the Lord said to Moses: Speak to the Israelites and say to them: 'When you cross the Jordan into Canaan, designate some towns to be your cities of refuge, to which a person who has killed someone accidentally may flee. They will be places of refuge from the avenger, so that a person accused of murder may not die before he stands trial before the assembly.'"

André and Magda Trocmé

and the gospel, even if that loyalty requires disobeying the law. The second was that resisting violence by responding in kind is in effect collaboration with the enemy, because it contributes to the hatred and will-to-destroy that motivates the enemy. Only love of enemies and the renunciation of violence breaks the cycle.

Officials of the Vichy regime (think of Captain Louis Renault as played by Claude Rains in the film *Casablanca*) knew quite well what was going on in Le Chambon, but the villagers were so resourceful in eluding authorities that there was only one successful raid during the years in which Jews were given sanctuary. Daniel Trocmé, André's cousin and co-worker, refusing to let the children put in his care be taken away without him, was then also arrested and later died in Maidanek concentration camp in eastern Poland.

Everyone in the village risked arrest, imprisonment, and possible execution. The danger was acute because life-saving work on such a scale simply could not be hidden. What they did was an act of collective heroism on an extraordinary scale, and yet those who did it were quite ordinary people.[3]

André Trocmé nearly paid with his life when, in the winter of 1943, he was arrested. He was out visiting parishioners in remote farms when the police, after cutting telephone lines into Le Chambon and stationing guards at key locations around the town, arrived at his house. Hours passed. By the time Trocmé returned, the evening meal was ready. Magda insisted her husband be given time to eat, then invited the police to join the family at the table. Meanwhile seven Jews were nervously in hiding in the attic.

The police presence at the Trocmé house was quickly discovered by the villagers who little by little gathered outside the presbytery to offer their farewells. When André stepped from the house, his neighbors embraced their pastor and gave him packets containing precious gifts in those times of extreme austerity: candles, warm socks, chocolate, biscuits, a tin of sardines, even a sausage. One of the police officers said, "I have never seen such a farewell, never." Like so many others at that moment, Trocmé too was weeping. In his official police report of the arrest, the arresting officer dared to say that the people of Le Chambon were "full of love." As Trocmé was taken away, one woman began to sing "A Mighty Fortress Is Our God." The hymn was taken up by the entire village.

Trocmé refused to deny that he was sheltering Jews and also refused to sign a declaration promising to obey the law. "These people came here for help and for shelter," he told the Vichy authorities. "I am their shepherd. A shepherd does not forsake his flock. I do not know what a Jew is. I know only human beings." Remarkably, André Trocmé was freed after four weeks of imprisonment. Perhaps his captors didn't quite know what to do with him—perhaps some sympathized.

Twice our family has gone as pilgrims to Le Chambon. It was years since André Trocmé's death, and still more since he was the town's pastor, yet older people still spoke of Pastor Trocmé's long

---

3. The story of "how goodness happened" at Le Chambon is told in detail in Philip Hallie, *Lest Innocent Blood Be Shed* (New York: Harper & Row, 1979).

walks through snow and rain to visit the sick, and still remembered his sermons.

"I especially remember his preaching about the parable of the Good Samaritan," said an old farmer. "That story became the way we lived in those years. The people we took in or helped across the Swiss border, for us these people were ones who had been stripped and beaten and left at the side of the road to die. How could we not open our homes to them? How could we say no to them and call ourselves Christians? How could we even keep the Bible in our house and not accept them, too?"

It was one of the small miracles of the war that Trocmé survived his imprisonment and lived on for many years, remaining deeply engaged in peace work and pastoral service until the end of his life. "There is no *way* to peace," he said in one much-quoted sermon. "Peace is the way."[4]

His wife, Magda, who died in 1996, was still alive at the time of my last visit to Le Chambon. She remained the sort of person who wouldn't hesitate to invite her enemies to sit at the family table. It surprises her, in fact, that anyone could imagine *not* feeding their enemies. "They have to eat, too," she said as we ate lunch. "You must remember that usually what they do is only because they are afraid. They don't want to do it—in fact they are ashamed. But they are afraid of what will happen to them if they say no."

4. The American peace campaigner A. J. Muste used Trocmé's words so often that the text has often been attributed to him.

The Whirlpool of War

IF WE ARE BETTER to understand the obstacles to loving one's enemy, among the questions to explore is what is it that drives so many people, including Christians, to take an active part in war?

Certainly there are those for whom it is a matter of deep conviction. On every side each war has its committed volunteers.

Others join because they see it as their patriotic duty—for them it is unthinkable to do otherwise: "I am [fill in the blank with one's national identity], and I do what my nation requires of me."

Times of national trauma, such as the 9/11 attack on the World Trade Center, draw many to volunteer for military service. "Signing up was a kind of substitution for the victims' lives," as one friend put it before being sent to fight in Iraq.

For many who put on a military uniform a key motivating factor is fear of being thought a coward should they not do so. In Britain at the start of the First World War, Admiral Charles Fitzgerald founded "The Order of the White Feather." The idea was that patriotic women would present men not in uniform with a white feather as a means of shaming them into enlisting. Remarkably the women who took up the campaign included prominent feminists and suffragettes, among them Emmeline Pankhurst and her daughter Christabel. The white-feather method proved very effective.

For some, military service gives the abandonment of an unpleasant or boring domestic life a noble façade: "Sorry, dear, but I'm leaving home to serve my country."

There are also those eager to have a license to possess and use deadly weapons and who seek a part in the ultimate death-risking, life-taking adventure.

Many—in times of economic crisis a great many—join as a means of escape from joblessness or being trapped in society's lowest economic tier. Countless young men and women have gone to war in recent years because being in the military was a ladder up from the bottom—a job, respect, education, vocational training, a possible military career, or at least preparation for employment in civilian life.

And there are those—I was one of them—who sign up because they find military service an attractive first step into adulthood: travel, room and board, free medical care, and, at the same time, being on one's own at least some of the time. In my case I was drawn by posters and folders that were headlined "Join the Navy and See the World." (My period of Navy service brought me to exotic Illinois, New Jersey, and Washington, DC. As it happened, I never spent a single minute afloat, not even in a Navy rowboat.)

For everyone, soldier and civilian alike, propaganda plays a major role. Wars are not only fought but marketed as carefully and cleverly as any commercial product. Slogans abound—"the war to end all wars," "a war to make the world safe for democracy," "the war on terror." Propaganda, often presented as news, delivers an education in enmity while at the same time providing the war at hand with moral wrapping.

Recent wars have been sold as human rights missions. Thus the war against Iraq, to give one recent example, allegedly had nothing to do with money, oil, or Western strategic interests, but was presented as a project to save the Iraqi people from a tyrant (in fact regime change has made life worse for war survivors in Iraq) plus a preemptive means of defending the world from Iraqi weapons of mass destruction (it turned out there were none).

Recruiting poster

Not least, there is the part played by peer-group pressure. One of the major lessons in my early adult life was becoming aware of how readily we shape ourselves to fit into the society we happen to belong to and often to do so unconsciously.

I learned this fact of life in the early 1960s as a consequence of one of the routine activities that was an element of Catholic Worker life in New York, a community I joined after obtaining an early discharge from the Navy as a conscientious objector. Once a week several of us would go uptown to hand out leaflets critical of preparations for nuclear war. In those days, the open-air testing of nuclear weapons was frequent. In expectation of nuclear war, people were encouraged to build underground shelters or, for those in cities, to take shelter in designated places. We few would stand for an hour at mid-day on the four corners of a Lexington Avenue intersection in the immediate neighborhood of the office responsible for "civil defense," the organizing center for all that New Yorkers were obliged to do in preparing for a nuclear attack. Our simple message was that you are not likely to survive nuclear war by taking shelter in the subways or entering a shelter under your backyard, but if by any chance you did survive, you would find yourself in a world so devastated that you would envy the dead.

It was an education attempting to connect with people hurrying along a busy city street. New York's traffic light system being what it is, people come down the avenues in waves. I quickly learned that the response of the first person in each group almost always determined the response of everyone who happened to be following him even though they were all strangers to one another. Not a word was said, not a look was exchanged—the process was automatic and unconscious. This meant that I had to do my very best to get the man in front (almost always it was a man) to take the flyer. If I succeeded, at least some of those behind him were likely to follow his example. If he refused, the chances were no one in that group would accept the piece of paper I was offering. If he balled up the leaflet and threw it on the ground, some of those following him were likely to do the same. My best hope was to make eye contact with the front runner. This requires what a nun friend of mine calls "hospitality of the face."

What I learned on Lexington Avenue is that we're just as bound together as the varieties of fish that swim in schools and animals that band together in herds. It's a human tendency to shape our lives, activities, opinions, and vocabularies according to what is more or less "normal" among the people we happen to be living and working with or wish to be accepted by. With rare exceptions, we adjust our lives, even our understanding and

Dorothy Day with a poster

practice of Christianity, to fit within the norms of the society we're part of. Thus, if I had been living in Germany in the 1930s and didn't have well-formed convictions that put me on guard about Nazism, the chances are I would have held Hitler in high regard, said "Heil Hitler" when it was expected, and perhaps even become a card-carrying Nazi. Or if I had grown up in a racist milieu, it would be remarkable if I didn't become a racist myself. If everyone in the neighborhood puts the national flag by their front door, would I dare to isolate myself by not doing the same? Go to a windy place and you notice how the trees are shaped by the wind. It takes courage and a carefully formed conscience for your thoughts, words, and actions not to be shaped by whatever group you are part of. If the group is pro-war, chances are I will be too and will play a supportive or, if pressed, active role in war, including actual killing.

Napoleon as Role Model

BUT WHAT ABOUT KILLING done apart from war—killing in the sense of premeditated homicide? Jesus is concerned not only with *acts* of deadly violence but with the intellectual, psychological, and spiritual events that suppress conscience and set the stage for killing.

In *Crime and Punishment*, the Russian novelist Dostoevsky explores how aversion turns to hatred and hatred to murder. The central figure in the novel is an intelligent but bitter student, Raskolnikov. In debt to a miserly old woman in St. Petersburg, he spends long hours imagining how, through a single act of violence, he might not only free himself from debt but obtain the money he knows she keeps hidden in a chest under her bed, making (he is convinced) far better use of it than did the miser. He imagines using the treasure in ways that will be "salutary to mankind." What right, anyway, does such a wicked old woman have to life?

He knows that all of society's moral codes and laws stand against murder. Needing to rationalize the act he dreams of committing, Raskolnikov finds justification in the example of Napoleon. It was Napoleon's superhuman greatness, he decides, that freed him from the restrictions of ordinary morality. In the name of national glory, Napoleon was able to kill without limit, and yet no one called him a murderer. Napoleon "destroys Toulon, butchers Paris, forgets an army in Egypt, expends half-a-million men in the Moscow campaign, shakes himself free with a pun in Vilnius, and when he is dead, they put up monuments to him." Raskolnikov concludes that he is just as free as Napoleon to kill. Like so many before him, he has found a philosophical justification for taking life.

Finally Raskolnikov not only commits the murder he planned but another he didn't intend: he kills a young retarded woman,[1] an

---

1. Dostoevsky describes her as a *yurodivi*, the Russian term for a holy fool, a category of sanctity.

innocent bystander who happened to witness the crime. In fact violent actions rarely go as planned. In the dehumanized vocabulary of war, it's now called "collateral damage."

In Dostoevsky's scrutiny of the intellectual and spiritual life of Raskolnikov in the days preceding the actual killing, the reader realizes that Raskolnikov has already become a murderer even while his victims are alive and well. Within himself Raskolnikov has crossed the border into hell—the hell of isolating himself in a loveless void. As the monk Father Zosima says in Dostoevsky's last novel, *The Brothers Karamazov*, "What is hell? I maintain that it is the suffering of being unable to love."[2]

Eventually, the two murders having been committed and all that he has stolen safely hidden, Raskolnikov finds he has gotten away with his crime. No incriminating evidence is found nor is there any witness who can testify against him. Yet far from being relieved, Raskolnikov descends into a storm of doubt about what he has done. His rationalizations are eaten away by guilt. In the end he confesses his crimes, paying the price of many years of exile and hard labor in Siberia. For all its elements of detective fiction, *Crime and Punishment* is ultimately not so much a book about crime as about conversion and repentance.

For Dostoevsky, the figure of Raskolnikov as murderer is not that of an exceptional person but rather of a heightened image of nihilistic modern man and woman, desperate to possess and control, distressed about injustice but in a state of radical alienation from others and from God.

Dostoevsky's insights are not new. In the Sermon on the Mount, Jesus reminds his listeners of the prohibition of killing in the Ten Commandments and the truth that every destructive action has unseen roots within us: "But I say to you that everyone who is angry with his brother shall be liable to judgment . . . and whoever says 'You fool!' shall be liable to the fire of hell" (Matthew 5:21-22).

The fire of hell is often one's burning conscience.

---

2. Fyodor Dostoevsky, *The Brothers Karamazov*, trans. Richard Pevear and Larissa Volokhonsky (New York: Everyman's Library, Alfred A. Knopf, 1992), Book VI, Chapter 3.

Reconciliation before Communion

So FUNDAMENTAL IS RESPECT for the lives of others in the teaching of Jesus that he sees worship of God or the reception of communion at a eucharistic service as incompatible with rancor or animosity of any kind. In the Sermon on the Mount, he says,

> So, if you are offering your gift at the altar and there remember that your brother has something against you, leave your gift there before the altar and go; first be reconciled with your brother, and then come and offer your gift. (Matthew 5:23-24)

In the oldest rite of worship still used in Christianity, the liturgy attributed to Saint John Chrysostom, an archbishop of Constantinople in the fourth century, the service begins with the words "Blessed is the Kingdom of the Father and the Son and the Holy Spirit," followed by the solemn summons, "In peace let us pray to the Lord." This is the first petition of the Litany of Peace, a litany one hears in all services at every Orthodox church in the world.

Peace is not only a goal but a precondition of worship, for how can we pray as a community if we are divided by enmity? How can we be part of a service in which we seek eucharistic communion with God if we are out of communion with one another?

In the communal worship of the early church, the concluding action of the first half of the service, the Liturgy of the Catechumens, was the exchange of the kiss of peace, a physical gesture to demonstrate no one present was infected with enmity. Vestiges of this rite still survive in many churches.

One of the remarkable aspects of the early church was its emphasis on Christians being at all times in a state of peace not only with fellow believers and friends but with those who threatened their lives. Even after the Emperor Constantine allied himself with Christianity, the church regarded people who had taken human life as having barred themselves from communion, to which they could return only after an extended period of rigorous penance. The emphasis was on conversion of enemies, not their death. As Saint John Chrysostom preached,

> *It is certainly a finer and a more wonderful thing to change the mind of enemies and to bring them to another way of thinking than to kill them (especially when they were only Twelve and the world was full of wolves). We ought to be ashamed of ourselves, we who act so very differently [than the Apostles] and rush like wolves upon our foes. So long as we are sheep, we have the victory; but if we are wolves, we are beaten—for then the help of the shepherd is withdrawn from us, for he feeds sheep not wolves.... [And can violent people dare to receive communion?] What excuse shall we have if, eating of the Lamb [of Christ], we become as wolves? If, led like sheep into pasture, we behave as though we were ravening lions? This mystery [of the Eucharist] requires that we should be innocent not only of violence but of all enmity, however slight, for this is the mystery of peace.*[1]

Down through the centuries countless Christians, many of them later canonized, have lived as sheep among wolves, in the process bringing many, even whole nations, to conversion.

One finds pastors in our own time with a similar understanding of the church. One remarkable example is Archbishop Elias Chacour of Haifa. Not only among Palestinians, both Christian and Muslim, but among many Jews, he has become one of the most respected religious leaders of northern Israel.

At the time I met him he was simply Father Elias, priest of Ibillin, an ancient hilltop village between Haifa and Nazareth in Galilee. Olive trees surround Ibillin, some of them called "Roman trees," meaning that they have been growing where they stand at least since the Roman occupation and thus are as old as Christianity. Today

---

1. Homilies on Matthew, XXXIII; translation from Donald Attwater, *St. John Chrysostom: Pastor and Preacher* (London: Harvill Press, 1959), 72.

Fr. Elias Chacour

the parish Father Elias led before he was made bishop is still thriving. There is a regional high school, a community center, and a large library. In the library entrance way is a beautifully made sign in Arabic with this text from the writings of the sixth-century abbot Saint Dorotheos of Gaza:

> *God is the creator of all human beings, with their differences, their colors, their races, their religions. Be attentive: Every time you draw nearer to your neighbor, you draw nearer to God. Be attentive: Every time you go farther from your neighbor, you go farther from God.*

When Father Elias was first sent to that town, there was no community center or library, and parish members, though living side by side, were far apart. The church building was falling down, and the small congregation that gathered inside was in no better condition than the building. During his first night in Ibillin no one even offered their new pastor the use of a guest bed—he had to sleep in his small Volkswagen.

"When the people were assembled in the church," Father Elias told me, "the divisions that ran through the parish could be seen in the way the people arranged themselves—four distinct groups, each keeping a distance from the others, and everyone with grim faces. The empty space between the four groups made the sign of the Cross."

"The fundamental division in the church," he explained, "was between four brothers. Even the death of their mother had not provided the occasion for the brothers to be in the same room together."

On Palm Sunday of his first year at Ibillin, Father Elias looked from the front of the church at the stony faces before him. One of the brothers, a policeman, sat in the front row with his wife and children.

"There were readings from the Bible, but all the while the congregation endured me indifferently," Elias recalled. "They were fulfilling their holy day obligation to warm the benches, nothing more." But before the service ended, he did something no one had anticipated. After the Gospel reading, when it was time for the sermon, he walked to the back of the church and padlocked the door.

Returning to the front of the church, he told his parishioners,

Sitting in this building does not make you a Christian. You are a people divided. You argue and hate one another. You gossip and spread lies. Your religion is a lie. If you can't love your brother whom you see, how can you say that you love God who is invisible? You have allowed the Body of Christ to be disgraced. I have tried for months to unite you. I have failed. I am only a man. But there is someone else who can bring you together in true unity. His name is Jesus Christ. He has the power to forgive you. So now I will be quiet and allow him to give you that power. If you will not forgive, then

we stay locked in here. If you want, you can kill each other. In that
case I'll provide your funerals gratis.

"How long," I asked, "was the silence that followed?" "I don't know," he replied. "I didn't dare look at my watch. Perhaps only ten minutes, perhaps twenty. It seemed like hours. But at last the policeman stood up, faced the congregation, bowed his head and said, 'I am sorry. I am the worst of all. I have hated my own brothers. I have hated them so much that I wanted to kill them. More than any of you, I need forgiveness.'" He turned to Father Elias. "Father, can you forgive me?" "Come here," Father Elias replied. They embraced each other with the kiss of peace. "Now go and greet your brothers." The four brothers rushed together, meeting halfway down the aisle, and in tears forgave each other. "In an instant," Father Elias recalled, "the church was a chaos of embracing and repentance."

Father Elias had to shout to make his next words audible. "Dear friends, we are not going to wait until next week to celebrate the Resurrection. Let us begin it now. We were dead to each other. Now we are alive again." He began to sing the paschal hymn, "Christ is risen from the dead, trampling down death by death, and on those in the tombs bestowing life." The congregation joined in the hymn. Unchaining the door, Elias led them into the village streets. "For the rest of the day and far into the evening, I joined groups of believers as they went from house to house. At every door, someone had to ask forgiveness for a certain wrong. Never was forgiveness withheld. It was a resurrection for the entire village. All that we achieved in the years that followed had its roots in that Palm Sunday."[2]

---

2. Author interview with Fr. Elias Chacour; see also Elias Chacour, *Blood Brothers* (Grand Rapids, MI: Chosen Books, 1984, 2003).

Active Love

IT IS THE UNSENTIMENTAL biblical understanding of love that the saintly monk Father Zosima speaks of in Dostoevsky's last novel, *The Brothers Karamazov*. Father Zosima, a Russian Orthodox monk nearing the end of his life, is daily sought by pilgrims who seek his blessing and advice. Mainly they are poor peasants, many of whom have walked long distances to reach the monastery, but some live comfortable lives. On this occasion Father Zosima is confronted by a wealthy woman racked with doubt about the existence of God. She asks how she can find certainty in matters of faith.

Father Zosima responds that no explanation or argument can achieve this, only the practice of "active love." His advice is simple: "Try to love your neighbors actively and tirelessly. The more you succeed in loving, the more you'll be convinced of the existence of God and the immortality of your soul. And if you reach complete selflessness in the love of your neighbor, then undoubtedly you will believe, and no doubt will even be able to enter your soul. This has been tested. It is certain."

The woman responds with the confession that she sometimes dreams about a life of loving service to others—she even imagines herself becoming a Sister of Mercy, living in holy poverty, serving the poor in the humblest way. It seems to her such a wonderful thought that tears come to her eyes. But then it crosses her mind how ungrateful some of the people she would be serving are likely to be. They will probably complain that the soup she is serving isn't hot or thick enough, the bread isn't fresh enough, the bed is too hard and the covers too thin. She confesses to Zosima that she couldn't bear such ingratitude—and so her dreams about serving others vanish, and once again she finds herself wondering if there really is a God.

To this Zosima responds with four sentences worth memorizing:

Active love is a harsh and fearful thing compared with love in dreams. Love in dreams thirsts for immediate action, rapidly performed and with everyone watching. Indeed it will go so far as the giving even of one's life, provided it does not take long and everyone is looking on and praising. Whereas active love is labor and perseverance.[1]

Zosima's advice is not just for the few. Look around. Countless people are engaged in active love every day of their lives, doing work that in one way or another helps sustain the lives of others, from children to the aged, from neighbors to strangers.

One of the people who, in a remarkable way, centered her life on practicing active love was Dorothy Day, co-founder of the Catholic Worker movement. Her sources of inspiration were many, but one was the influence Dostoevsky's novels had in shaping her understanding of Christianity. Late in her life, during her only visit to Russia, one of her principal acts of pilgrimage was to pray at Dostoevsky's grave in St. Petersburg (Leningrad in the Soviet period). She first read *The Brothers Karamazov* when she was a high school student. Later in life she would occasionally recite from memory key passages from the text. It was no surprise to her when she discovered that Father Zosima was in part modeled on a monk Dostoevsky knew personally: Father Amvrosi, Elder of the Optina monastery in central Russia.[2] For Dorothy Day, Father Zosima was as real as an old friend sitting at her side.

In 1933, in the midst of the Great Depression, Dorothy Day both founded a publication and started a lay movement, the Catholic Worker, that was meant for anyone, whether married or unmarried, young or old. A few months after the first issue of the *Catholic Worker* appeared, the first of many houses of hospitality opened

1. Dostoevsky, *Brothers Karamazov*, Book VI, Chapter 3.
2. Staretz [Elder] Amvrosi of Optina was recognized as a saint by the Russian Orthodox Church in 1988. I had the privilege of being present for his canonization. For details of his life, see http://en.wikipedia.org/wiki/Ambrose_of_Optina.

During the Depression,
lining up for soup at the
Catholic Worker

its doors. Today there are hundreds. The *Catholic Worker* sold, and
still sells, for a penny a copy—priced to be affordable for those out
of work. Dorothy's first editorial said the new paper would show its
readers that the church is concerned not only with each person's
spiritual well-being but also with their material welfare. The paper
caught on. By the end of the first year there were many thousands of
subscribers.

From the start, Catholic Worker houses of hospitality were places
of welcome for the down-and-out. There were no forms to fill out or
sermons to endure while you ate your soup and bread. No programs
of self-improvement were imposed on those who came through the
door. The Catholic Worker, in common with the Holy Rule of Saint
Benedict, believed that "each person should be received as Christ."

Dorothy was sometimes criticized for her non-institutional
approach to hospitality. A social worker visiting the Catholic Worker
house in New York once asked Dorothy how long "clients" were
"allowed" to stay. "We let them stay forever," Dorothy replied some-

what testily. "They live with us, they die with us, and we give them a
Christian burial. We pray for them after they are dead. Once they are
taken in, they become members of the family. Or rather they always
were members of the family. They are our brothers and sisters in
Christ."[3]

Dorothy Day underwent two decisive conversions in her life, the
first to the poor, the second to Christ. The first—sparked first by
reading and then by life experience—began in her teens. At age nineteen, she had her first job as a reporter for a New York-based radical
newspaper, *The Call*, and rented the first of many tiny apartments
in slum neighborhoods in lower Manhattan. Still nineteen, she was
arrested and jailed for the first time, the youngest participant in an
all-women suffragist demonstration in front of the White House.

Eleven years later, in 1927, soon after becoming a mother, she
was received into the Catholic Church, a step that bewildered
some friends and scandalized others for whom religion was deception. It took her five years to fully connect both conversions. The
result was the Catholic Worker movement, which—as co-founder
Peter Maurin said—sought "to build a new society within the shell
of the old."

At the core of the Catholic Worker way of life are the works of
mercy: feeding the hungry, giving drink to the thirsty, clothing
the naked, giving shelter to the homeless, caring for the sick, visiting those in prison. In fact, each of the works of mercy is simply an
aspect of hospitality. All six are cited by Christ in his only account of
the Last Judgment as recorded by Matthew in the twenty-fifth chapter of his Gospel. "What you have done to the least person," Jesus
declares, "you have done to me" (Matthew 25:45).

Dorothy sought an integrated way of life in which nothing one did
was at odds with nurturing and saving lives. This led her to oppose
participation in war. "We see that the works of mercy oppose the
works of war," she said.

---

3. Jim Forest, *All Is Grace: A Biography of Dorothy Day* (Maryknoll, NY: Orbis
Books, 2011), 336.

The works of mercy call us to feed the hungry, but war creates hunger. We are required to clothe the naked, but war burns the skin from people's bodies. We are called to welcome the homeless, but war creates millions of refugees. We are called to take care of the sick, but even sickness is a weapon in war. We are called to visit the prisoner, but war makes thousands into prisoners of war. We would rather be with Our Lord in prison than killing him on a battlefield.[4]

Her antiwar stance made her a frequent target of criticism. Dom Helder Camara, a Brazilian bishop who had a great deal in common with Dorothy Day, faced similar condemnations for similar activi-

---

4. For an extensive online collection of the writings of Dorothy Day, see http://dorothyday.catholicworker.org/index.html.

ties. "When I give bread to the hungry," he remarked, "they call me a saint. When I ask why the hungry have no bread, they call me a Communist." Certainly that happened to Dorothy, although she rejected Communist ideology and had no interest in political parties. She was political only in the broad sense that she could not live in peace with a social order that caused so much hunger, homelessness, and suffering. She was political in the sense that she understood that the gospel has to do with life as a whole, not only with how we worship on Sundays but how we live together each day of our lives.

Perhaps more than any Catholic since Saint Francis of Assisi, Dorothy Day began a process that restored awareness that the Sermon in the Mount—chapters 4, 5, and 6 of Matthew's Gospel—is a text meant for all Christians and not only clerics, monks, and nuns.

When Dorothy died on November 29, 1980, it was a widely marked event, noticed not only by Catholics but Christians of every variety, many people in other religious traditions, and some who stood outside religion. In 1997 the Archdiocese of New York marked the hundredth anniversary of Dorothy's birth by launching a process that may in time result in her canonization.

"Why does the church canonize saints?" Cardinal John O'Connor asked on that occasion. "In part, so that their person, their works, and their lives will become that much better known, and that they will encourage others to follow in their footsteps—and so the Church may say, 'This is sanctity, this is the road to eternal life.'" Dorothy was, he said, someone who believed that a person is "a temple of God, sacred, made in the image and likeness of God, infinitely more important in its own way than any building. . . . To Dorothy Day, everyone was a cathedral."

The Vatican has since given her the title "Servant of God Dorothy Day" and may in time add her name to the calendar of saints. Whether or not canonization ever occurs, countless people revere her memory and live more adventurous lives of faith because of the example she gave of overcoming enmity in a life of active love and hospitality.

Part II

Nine Disciplines of Active Love

In the opening pages of this book we asked the question, "How does a conversion of heart take place?" All these stories and examples serve to help show us the way. But how do we acquire the kind of active love that helps us overcome enmity?

Drawing on the New Testament, we can identify nine disciplines of active love that are aspects of personal and group response to enmity:

1. praying for enemies
2. doing good to enemies
3. turning the other cheek
4. forgiveness
5. breaking down the dividing wall of enmity
6. refusing to take an eye for an eye
7. seeking nonviolent alternatives
8. practicing holy disobedience
9. recognizing Jesus in others

The pages that follow will reflect on each of these disciplines.

Praying for Enemies

"But I say to you love your enemies *and pray for those who persecute you*" (Matthew 5:44). In a single sentence Jesus links love of enemies with prayer for them. In fact, prayer is the essential first step without which love of enemies would be hardly possible.

If we have any interest in attempting to love our enemies, a necessary starting point is to admit we have enemies and, insofar as we can, to be able to identify them by name. Once I have admitted to myself that I have enemies, I have a starting point. Until then, the Gospel commandment to love one's enemies and pray for them is a dead letter.

Situations of enmity exist in everyone's daily life: at home, at work, at school, between neighbors. If you have teenage children, surely you've experienced them looking at you with eyes that explode with hatred, an animosity that could well be mirrored in your own eyes. Pick up a newspaper—page after page contains vivid reminders of how much enmity and violence surround us. In the same pages we see what the cost is in suffering, despair, and death. You find conflict even in monasteries. I once watched two young Benedictine novices silently battle with each other by arranging and rearranging the salt-and-pepper shakers that stood on the refectory table between them. Those small containers became warring chess pieces.

We don't need to travel far to find adversarial relationships, yet most of us are reluctant to use the word "enemy" in describing people who are part of our daily lives.

I have an exercise for you. You'll need a piece of paper and something to write with.

Stop for a few minutes and think about people you know who make you feel anger or fear, persons you dislike and whose company you avoid, individuals in your family, neighborhood, workplace, or church whom it distresses you to see, individuals who have hurt you or hurt those in your care. Think of people you would prefer not to pray for. People you find outrageous.

Also think about groups or categories of people you think of by national, racial, political, or religious label. Think of people who are the current or potential targets of weapons and armies that in some way you support, passively or actively, willingly or unwillingly, through your work, political alignments, payment of taxes, or other activities.

As names occur to you, pause to write them down. Do so even if you think the word "enemy" is too strong. In instances in which you haven't got a name, use a label.

Okay, now you have a first draft of a prayer list. Try to refer to it on a daily basis.

Look again at what you have written down. Think about each name or label. In each case, picture an individual face or, in the case of labels, an appropriate image. Give yourself at least a minute for each name or label. Insofar as you are able, consider in each case how the enmity began. Consider incidents or reasons that explain or justify your feelings. Consider ways in which the enmity involved has shaped, limited, damaged, or endangered your life or the lives of people dear to you.

Next step. Try and take the point of view of those you have listed. Are they actually your enemies? Or might it be truer to say you're their enemy? Or is it half and half? In either case, what have you done or failed to do that might explain or justify their hostility?

Now a potentially embarrassing question: You're a Christian. Christ has told you to pray for your enemies. When have you prayed for any of the people on your list? Regularly? Occasionally? Rarely? Never?

Have you searched for points of common ground and possible agreement? Have you allowed yourself to be aware of qualities that are admirable in those you have listed or have you preferred to see only what, from your perspective, is flawed in them?

Consider what might happen to you, to others, if this enmity continues: separation, divorce, court battles, children caught in the crossfire, shattered friendships, division in your parish, division among co-workers, misery in the work place, loss of employment. . . .

In the case of differences between nations, think of ways in which you participate in enmities that, if they worsen, could explode into war. In a world in which there are thousands of nuclear weapons and other weapons of mass destruction, consider what war might mean in the worst case. Are you doing anything that might make war less likely or helping bring to an end a war in progress?

Prayer that doesn't influence your own actions means little. Why should God pay attention to a prayer that has little or no influence on your own behavior? What steps have you taken to change relationships with those on your list? Have you talked to others who might help or intervene in a constructive way? Can you imagine what you could do that might help bring to an end any of the enmities you have listed? What can you do that might help convert enmity to friendship?

The church, in recognizing saints, places before us many models of sanctity—people who, in a wide variety of ways, also had to deal with enemies. By taking time to study the lives of particular saints, we are likely to find helpful models.

Here's an example. One of the masters of the spiritual life in the past century was Saint Silouan the Athonite, an uneducated Russian peasant who was born in 1866 and died in 1938. In his youth he was an immensely strong man who had a volcanic temper. During a feast day celebrating the patron saint of his village, he was playing a concertina when two brothers, both cobblers, began to tease him. The older of the brothers tried to snatch the concertina from Silouan and a fight broke out between them.

"At first I thought of giving in to the fellow," Silouan told another monk later in his life,

> but then I was ashamed at how the girls would laugh at me, so I gave him a great hard blow in the chest. His body shot away and he fell backward with a heavy thud in the middle of the road. Froth and blood trickled from his mouth. All the onlookers were horrified. So was I. "I've killed him," I thought, and stood rooted

to the spot. For a long time the cobbler lay where he was. It was
over half an hour before he could rise to his feet. With difficulty
they got him home, where he was bad for a couple of months, but
he didn't die.[1]

For the rest of his life Silouan felt that there was only the slightest difference between himself and a murderer. He had yielded to a murderous impulse. It was only by chance that his powerful blow hadn't been deadly. Perhaps it's not surprising that, as time passed, he found himself drawn to a life of prayer and penance. After becoming a monk on Mount Athos, a Greek peninsula dotted with monasteries that juts into the Aegean Sea, he thought long and hard about violence and its causes, in the course of which he developed a profound sense of human interconnectedness. He realized that "through Christ's love, everyone is made an inseparable part of our own, eternal existence . . . for the Son of Man has taken within himself all mankind."

One need not be a contemplative monk in a remote monastery to be overwhelmed by a sense of human interconnection. I often think of Apollo 9 astronaut Russell Schweickart, who put into words a similar sense of human oneness that hit him as he looked through a window of his spacecraft:

You see the Earth not as something big . . . [but] as a small thing
out there. And the contrast between that bright blue and white
Christmas tree ornament and the black sky, that infinite universe,
really comes through, and the size of it, the significance of it. It is so
small and fragile and such a precious little spot in that universe that
you can block it out with your thumb, and you realize that on that
small spot, that little blue and white thing, is everything that means
anything to you—all of history, and music and poetry and art and
death and birth and love, all the tears, joy, games, all of it on that
little spot out there that you can cover with your thumb. And you

---

1. Archimandrite Sophrony, *Saint Silouan the Athonite* (Essex: Monastery of St. John the Baptist, 1991), 14-15.

*realize from that perspective that you've changed, that there's some-
thing new there, that the relationship is no longer what it was.*[2]

Saint Silouan had no spaceship window and probably could not
have imagined anyone flying to the moon, but the life of prayer provided him with the same discovery: there is one Earth; the borders
drawn on maps are invisible to the birds that fly over them; we really
are God's children; it really is one human family, and in God's eyes
the Earth is no bigger than a kitchen table.

Little by little Silouan came to the realization that love of enemies
is not simply an option of Christian life, a possibility that few will
attempt and fewer still achieve, but is "the central criterion of true
faith and of real communion with God, the lover of souls, the lover
of humankind." Or, as he said on other occasions, "No one has ever
known God without having loved his enemies."

There is nothing new in this. The Gospel author Saint John said
the same: "Whoever says he loves God but hates his neighbor
is a liar" (1 John 4:20). Could anyone say it more simply or more
plainly? Hatred of anyone blockades communion with God.

But without prayer for enemies we are ill prepared to love them.
There is no starting point. Prayer itself is an act of relationship. The
moment I pray for someone, however reluctantly, I establish an intimate connection with that person. Even the smallest act of caring
that prayer involves is a major step toward love, an act of participating in God's love for that person. Prayer gives us a point of access
to God's love for those we would otherwise regard with disinterest,
irritation, fear, or active hostility.

If love of enemies begins with prayer for them, it may be that we
need to think freshly about the nature of prayer.

Among books that have helped me in the endless struggle to
become more compassionate, collections of photos such as *The
Family of Man* have been of special value. Meditating on images in
The Face of Prayer, I was impressed by the comments of the photog-
rapher Abraham Menashe:

_____

2. Russell Schweickart, "No Frames, No Boundaries": www.context.org/iclib/
ic03/schweick.

> *Prayer is a deeply personal act through which we commune, peti-*
> *tion, reach out, and give thanks. . . . Prayer is present in all aspects*
> *of life. . . . When we attend to prayer, its nature becomes known to*
> *us. We take refuge in stillness, and in our most naked state become*
> *receptive to a life force that nourishes, heals, and makes us whole*
> *again. To the extent that we have the courage to seek moments of*
> *solitude and listen to our inner voice, we will be guided by a light*
> *that lives in us. We will come to know a love that does not disap-*
> *point—peace the world does not offer.*[3]

Prayer is something that reveals itself only through prayer. Like the taste of an orange, we can know it only from the inside. As Menashe put it, "When we attend to prayer, its nature becomes known to us."

While the recitation of sacred texts is important in every religious tradition, an early discovery each person makes is that, while words help, prayer is far more than reciting words. It often involves no words at all, only an attentive silence.

Prayer is placing ourselves in the presence of God—so easy to say but often so hard to do. The mystery we identify as "God" is more than a word, and no definition of God (creator, sustainer, savior, ground of being, higher power, lover of humankind) is adequate. Biblical and theological texts depend on metaphors, the essential verbal tool for touching the borders of the unexplainable.

One of the metaphors for God used by Saint Symeon the New Theologian[4] was water:

---

3. Abraham Menashe, *The Face of Prayer* (New York: Knopf, 1980), Introduction.

4. Symeon the New Theologian (949-1022) is one of three saints of the Orthodox Church to have been given the title of Theologian; the others are Saint John the Evangelist and Saint Gregory Nazianzen. Born in Galatia and educated at Constantinople, Symeon became abbot of the monastery of Saint Mamas. "Theologian" was not applied to Symeon in the modern academic sense of theological scholarship, but to recognize someone who spoke from personal experience of God. One of his principal teachings was that humans could and should experience *theōria*—literally "contemplation of," or direct encounter with God.

God can be known to us in the same way that a man can see an endless ocean while standing at the shore at night and holding only a dimly lit candle. Do you think he can see much? In fact very little, almost nothing. Even so, he can see the water very well. He knows there is a vast ocean before him, the limits of which he cannot perceive. The same is true of our knowledge of God.[5]

Yet an ocean is less than a drop of water compared to God. Many metaphors are helpful; no metaphor is adequate. God is simultaneously both close and distant, both merciful and demanding, both just and forgiving, father but also mother, ever new yet ageless, unchanging and yet the fountainhead of change, a God both of deserts and waterfalls. Words and images can only help in our pilgrimage toward God. "He who follows words is destroyed," Thomas Merton told the novices in his care.

Using another metaphor, we might think of God as a weaver, in fact *the* weaver. All creation, from the book in your hand to the most remote galaxy, is part of that endless and ongoing weaving. You and I are part of the fabric and so are our enemies. To approach God is to discover connections, including the ways that I and my enemy are bound together like crisscrossing threads in the same tapestry. The moment we turn toward God the weaver, we turn toward a divine love that connects everyone, whether a nun caring for a dying beggar or a psychopath who has just raped and murdered a stranger. This is the economy of grace that Christ is describing when he speaks of rain and sunlight being given to all, not just the virtuous. We are part of an interconnected human unity in which our worst enemy also exists. This doesn't mean that God is indifferent to the sins we or our enemies commit, but we are nonetheless objects of God's life-giving love and benefit from the divine hope that we might yet become what God intended us to become.

A starting point in prayer is being honest with God: presenting our-

---

5. Saint Symeon the New Theologian, Oration 61, *Works*, quoted in Leonid Ouspensky, *Theology of the Icon*, Vol. 1 (Crestwood, NY: St. Vladimir's Seminary Press, 1992), 33.

selves as we are, not as we wish we were or as we think God wants us to be, not dressing up for God but standing before God as naked as Adam and Eve. As a passage in the *Philokalia* (a venerable Orthodox collection of texts on prayer and other aspects of Christian life) puts it:

> *If we truly wish to please God and to be friends with the most blessed of friendships, let us present our spirit naked to God. Let us not draw into it anything of this present world—no art, no thought, no reasoning, no self-justification—even though we should possess all the wisdom of this world.*[6]

If we're going to present our spirits naked to God, there is no need to pretend to God that we love an enemy in an affectionate sense. Better to communicate our actual feelings. Perhaps something like this:

> *God, you must know I can't stand [the name of whomever you are at enmity with]. I often wish him dead or at least wish he were miserable and far away. But I pray for him because you commanded me to pray for my enemies. Personally I don't actually want to do it but I do want to be one of your disciples and I am trying to be obedient to your words. Help me to see him as you see him. Let me glimpse your image in him. May I live in such a way that both of us can lay aside our hostility and forgive each other. May I at least not be an obstacle to his salvation. I admit I find it hard to want anything good for him—help me to want it, help me to pray for him.*

The simplest of prayers can also be used. You may find it helpful to recite the Jesus Prayer—"Lord Jesus Christ, Son of the living God, have mercy on me"—or a variation of it: "Lord Jesus Christ, Son of the living God, have mercy on [the name of someone on your enemies list]."

By the way, be patient. Expect no quick results or even slow results.

---

6. Saint John of Karpathos, from section 49 of "For the Encouragement of the Monks in India," included in *The Philokalia: The Complete Text*, compiled by Saint Nikodimos of the Holy Mountain and St. Makarios of Corinth (London: Faber & Faber, 1979), vol. 1, pp. 309-10.

You may pray for years for a person or group and see no changes at all, at least none that you were hoping for. (In fact, prayer for a change even in one's own behavior requires persistence.) In prayer for an enemy, at the very least there is a change in you—the creation of a bond of care for the other.

We are told by Christ to pray for our enemies, but prayer itself can be difficult. No matter what its focus, prayer sometimes reminds us of the undercurrent of our own religious doubts. Among the prayers in the Gospel for which I have a particular gratitude is this one: "Lord, I believe—help my unbelief" (Mark 9:24). The man who first said that at least had the advantage of standing face to face with Jesus. We live twenty centuries later, in a time when who Jesus was has become the subject of countless books about the "historical Jesus," books whose authors rarely agree with one another. Some even dismiss the Jesus of the New Testament as a legend or invention. Among authors who admit he must have existed, some regard Jesus as a vagabond rabbi who was executed for his radical ideas and was resurrected only in the sense that his stories and teachings survived and became the basis for a new religion.

Many writers have vandalized the Jesus of the Gospels. The most successful recent revision of Jesus' life is Dan Brown's novel *The Da Vinci Code*, in which we find a cloak-and-dagger Catholic Church that has spent twenty centuries using any means necessary to suppress the fact that Jesus married Mary Magdalene and became a father, numbering the kings of medieval France among his descendants. (Not much of an achievement.) Brown's book has sold millions of copies and was made into a big-budget film. Sadly, many have taken the author's bogus history seriously.

On top of all the misinformation about Jesus, for many people the word "God" is far from easy to use. Pronouncing these three letters produces a sound that is often without content rather than a bridge into the depthless reality of a mysterious creator "in whom we live and move and have our being" (Acts 17:28). The word "God," so often ill treated and carelessly used, can also trigger recollections of the grave sins committed in God's name by people in responsible positions in religious structures: inquisitions, torture, heretics burned, Crusades and other religious wars, priests and nuns who abused children, bishops who protected child abusers, etc. Christians have often betrayed Christ's most basic teachings. It can be an ongoing struggle to develop a sense of God that isn't stained by ecclesiastical abuses of the word "God."

Yet so much draws us toward the God who, as one prayer used throughout the Orthodox Church reminds us, "is everywhere present, filling all things, the treasury of blessings and the giver of life."[7] Beauty itself opens a door toward heaven. All beauty, from the microcosmic to the macrocosmic, bears witness to God. At the base of our souls is a tilt toward God. Saint Augustine was right in proclaiming, "You have made us for yourself, O God, and our hearts are restless until they rest in you."[8]

To pray wholeheartedly can become the most vital force in life, not only empowering us in countless ways, but, like an underground spring flowing through hidden channels, reaching others, including those we view as enemies.

In praying for enemies, we are not hurling holy thoughts at them or petitioning God to make them into copies of ourselves. Rather we are bringing our enemies into that part of ourselves that is deepest and most vulnerable. We are begging God for the good of those whom, at other times, we wished ill or wished to harm. In praying for enemies, we are asking God to use us for the well-being of those we fear.

At the same time, we are asking to see ourselves as we are seen by those who fear us, so that we can see enmity not only from our side but from the other side, for we not only have enemies—we are enemies. We would do well to pray not only for the conversion of our adversaries but for our own conversion. We ourselves may be harder to convert than our adversaries. The most needed conversion may be my own.

---

7. The full text of the prayer: "O Heavenly King, the comforter, the spirit of truth, who is everywhere present, filling all things, the treasury of blessings and the giver of life, come and abide in us and cleanse us from every impurity and save, O Gracious One, our souls."

8. Augustine, *Confessions*, Book I.

Doing Good to Our Enemies

PRAYER IS ESSENTIAL, but prayer is not enough. Jesus calls us not only to pray but to act. In the words of Christ, "*Do good* to those who hate you, bless those who curse you" (Luke 6:28). Far from being an alternative to action, prayer helps empower us to undertake acts we might otherwise have been incapable of doing. It is useless to expect God to do what we refuse to help achieve. If we want God to take a prayer seriously, we need to take it seriously ourselves.

Contrary to popular belief, Jesus' teaching about active love toward enemies was not new doctrine. We find in the Mosaic Law: "If you meet your enemy's ox or his donkey going astray, you shall bring it back to him. If you see the donkey of one who hates you lying under a burden, you shall refrain from leaving him with it" (Exodus 23:4-5).

In the same vein, the Mosaic Law forbids the destruction of the fruit trees of enemies or the poisoning of their wells. The book of Proverbs actually calls for positive acts of caring for the well-being of adversaries: "If your enemy is hungry, give him bread" (25:21). This was taken up and expanded by Saint Paul:

> Bless those who persecute you; bless and do not curse them. Rejoice with those who rejoice, weep with those who weep. Live in harmony with one another; do not be haughty, but associate with the lowly; never be conceited. Repay no one evil for evil, but take thought for what is noble in the sight of all. If possible, so far as it depends upon you, live peaceably with all. Beloved, never avenge yourselves, but leave it to the wrath of God; for it is written, "vengeance is mine, I will repay, says the Lord." No, if your enemy is hungry, feed him; if he is thirsty, give him drink; for by doing so you will heap burning

coals upon his head. Do not be overcome by evil, but overcome evil with good. (Romans 12:14-21)

You've read it once, now read it again more slowly. Paul is simply amplifying the basic teachings of Jesus. He does so without encouraging unrealistic expectations that peace can be obtained simply by one's own peaceable behavior, though it might. The suffering that the young church had experienced, despite the most exemplary behavior, was clear evidence that there was sometimes no defense at all against the evil done by others. Paul must have often recalled the stoning of Stephen, a merciful and innocent man whose death he had witnessed and which occurred with his consent; he may even have been among those throwing the stones (Acts 7:58-60).

Paul calls on Christians to live peaceably with others no matter how unpeaceful those others may be, and in no case to seek revenge. If vengeance is required, he says, that is God's business. But for followers of Jesus, far from striking back at those who strike us, we are to do what is "noble in the sight of all," responding with care and compassion to the needs of our enemies. In doing so, he says, we heap "burning coals" around the enemy's head. This is like the metaphorical "burning coal" with which God purified the mouth of the prophet Isaiah so that he could preach God's thoughts rather than his own (Isaiah 6:6). Good deeds done to enemies may similarly purify their thoughts and lead them in an entirely different direction.

In a commentary on the passage, the fourth-century biblical translator Saint Jerome remarks, "We are not to revile and condemn our enemy, as the world does, but rather we are to correct him and lead him to repentance, so that being won over to our good deeds, he may be softened by the fire of charity and may cease to be an enemy."[1]

Sometimes even the failed attempt to feed an enemy has good results. Alfred Hassler, a former secretary of an American peace

---

1. Saint Jerome, "Against the Pelagians" 1.30 (from Saint Jerome, *Dogmatic and Polemical Works,* trans. John N. Hritzu [Fathers of the Church: A New Translation 53; Washington, DC: Catholic University of America Press, 1965], 275).

group, the Fellowship of Reconciliation, told an amazing story of something that happened in the mid-1950s, shortly after the Korean War. There was a disastrous famine in China claiming the lives of millions. At the same time, China was shelling two islands, Quemoy and Matsu, forward military bases of Taiwan, a U.S. ally. Another war seemed about to start in Asia. The Cold War was at its most frozen. A popular slogan at the time was "the only good Red is a dead Red." Many Americans argued that the thing to do was to use nuclear weapons against China. In fact, behind closed doors this was what the Pentagon's Joint Chiefs of Staff were recommending to President Dwight Eisenhower.

The response of the Fellowship of Reconciliation was to launch a campaign for famine relief in China. At the time the United States had the largest surplus of food in its history, purchased by the government to support farm prices. In an effort to symbolize a U.S.-to-China relief effort, thousands of small cotton sacks were manufactured, not even as big as a postcard, with a drawstring at one end and, on the other, a mailing label addressed to Eisenhower. The message on the cards read, "If your enemy hungers, feed him. Send surplus grain to China." Supporters of the initiative put a spoonful of rice, wheat, oatmeal, or breakfast cereal in the sacks and mailed them to the White House.

Despite the fact that this campaign was going on during the McCarthy period, when anyone advocating peace risked being called a Communist, the campaign got a remarkably positive reception, with many churches taking part. There was even a story about the effort on the front page of the *New York Times*, complete with a photo of a mini-rice sack with its message to the president. But months passed, interest dropped off, and finally the Fellowship of Reconciliation gave it up. The White House "made no comment," as they say. No surplus grain was sent to China.

"Many in China died of hunger," Al Hassler told me, "while the U.S. surplus grain remained in storage. Not far from where I lived, hundreds of tons of it were stored in decommissioned Navy ships right on the Hudson River near West Point. When the wind was blowing in the right direction, you could actually hear the sound of rats eating grain."

"But that's not the end of the story," Hassler continued.

Twenty years later, I happened to meet Harold Stassen, a former Pennsylvania governor who had gone on to direct Eisenhower's Foreign Operations Administration. Stassen recognized my name and told me that the Fellowship of Reconciliation campaign, which we thought had been entirely ignored at the White House, had in fact been discussed at three separate cabinet meetings! At these same cabinet meetings there was discussion of the recommendation from the Joint Chiefs of Staff that the United States attack China. At the third meeting, Eisenhower turned to the cabinet member responsible for the Food for Peace Program and asked, "How many of those grain bags have come in?" The answer was 45,000 plus tens of thousands of letters. Eisenhower's response was to say to the Pentagon people that if that many Americans were trying to find a conciliatory solution with China, it wasn't time to launch a war with China. The proposal was vetoed. Of course there was no letter from Eisenhower thanking us for helping him make up his mind and there was no White House press conference to announce the decision not to go to war with China. For many years we thought our effort had been a complete failure. It was just a chance encounter that revealed to us that, while we had failed in one way, we had helped accomplish something else that saved millions of lives.[2]

The teaching to do good to enemies is often viewed as profoundly unrealistic, but in fact it's a teaching full of common sense. Unless we want to pave the way to a tragic future, we must search for opportunities through which we can demonstrate to an opponent our longing for an entirely different kind of relationship. An adversary's moment of need can provide that opening.

For example consider this instance of what is sometimes referred

---

2. Interview with Alfred Hassler by Jim Forest and Diane Leonetti, published in *Fellowship* magazine, September 1974; Fellowship of Reconciliation, Nyack, NY 10960. See photo on p. 174.

to as "earthquake diplomacy." It concerns Greece and Turkey, neighboring countries that for many decades had been bitter enemies often on the brink of war.

On August 17, 1999, Turkey experienced a massive earthquake that severely affected many towns and cities, with the industrial city of Izmit the most severely damaged. A second major earthquake occurred five days later. The official number of casualties was 17,000, although the actual number is thought to be more than double that. About a third-of-a-million people were left homeless. The shift in the fault line passed through the most industrialized and urban areas of Turkey, including oil refineries and major factories. Istanbul was also hard hit.

To the world's astonishment, Greece was the first country to pledge aid and support to Turkey. Within hours of the earthquake, senior staff of the Greek Ministry of Foreign Affairs contacted their Turkish counterparts, then dispatched personal envoys to Turkey. The Greek Ministry of Public Order sent in a rescue team of twenty-four people with trained rescue dogs plus fire-extinguishing planes to help put out the huge blaze at an oil refinery. Greek medical teams followed—doctors and nurses plus tents, ambulances, medicine, water, clothes, food, and blankets. The Greek Orthodox Church launched a major fund-raising campaign for humanitarian relief. Throughout Greece, the Ministry of Health set up units for blood donations. The five largest municipalities of Greece sent a joint convoy with aid. When the mayor of Athens came personally to visit earthquake sites, he was greeted at the Istanbul airport by the mayor.

Both Greece's official actions and the responses of ordinary Greeks were given wide coverage day after day in every newspaper and TV channel in Turkey. Turks were astounded by the compassionate Greek response to Turkey's disaster.

As it happened, just weeks after the Turkish disaster, on September 7, 1999, Athens was hit by a powerful earthquake, the most devastating natural disaster in Greece in twenty years. While the death toll was relatively low, the damage to buildings and the infrastructure in some of the city's northern and western suburbs was severe.

This time Turkey responded—in fact Turkish aid was the first to reach Athens from outside Greece's borders. Within thirteen hours a twenty-person rescue team was flown in by a military plane. The Greek consulates and embassy in Turkey had their phone lines jammed with Turks calling to find out whether they could donate blood. One Turk offered to donate his kidney for a "Greek in need."

The very last thing our enemies imagine is that we could wish them well or do them well. For decades Greek and Turkish military forces had faced each other in a state of high alert. In the wake of this series of earthquakes in the two countries, there was a change of spiritual climate—the sense that the time had come for a new understanding. Since 1999 there has been no talk of impending war between Turkey and Greece. A river of blood that might have flowed was prevented all because two countries decided to aid their enemy in a time of crisis.

One finds many examples of the love of enemies—love in the sense of doing for an enemy what you would do for a friend—not only in stories of saints on the church calendar but in the lives of people whom we know.

I often think of an event in the life of Metropolitan Anthony of Sourozh, for many years leader of the Russian Orthodox Church in England. A refugee from Russia, much of his youth and early adulthood had been spent in France, a country that became home for many fleeing the Bolshevik revolution and the civil war that followed. His higher education was in medicine. By the time Hitler's armies invaded France, he was an army surgeon stationed in a military hospital. In the course of his work he was given charge of a wounded German prisoner. Here is the way he spoke of it in an interview with Timothy Wilson:

> *In the hospital where I was working as a war surgeon, a German came in once with one finger smashed by a bullet. The head surgeon came round and looked at the finger and said "Take it off." That was a very quick and easy decision—amputation would take only five minutes. Then the German said, "Is there anyone here who can speak German?" I spoke with the man and discovered that he*

*was a watchmaker and if his finger was removed he would prob-
ably never be able to work again. So we spent five weeks treating
his smashed finger and he was able to leave the hospital with five
fingers instead of only four. From this encounter I learned the fact
that, for him, being a watchmaker was as important as anything
else. I would say that I learnt to put human concerns first.*[3]

Nothing is more blinding than war, an event in which dehumanizing the enemy becomes a psychological necessity. The more human
our perception of an adversary, the harder it is to cause him harm.
Even in times of peace, as we might use the word in a minimalist
way to mean "a time without war," it's no easy thing to see others as
human beings rather than beings who are first of all the bearers of a
nationality or religion, or as people defined according to their social
role.

In this case the wounded man was a soldier of an invading army,
the worst kind of uninvited visitor, and here is a young army physi-
cian ignoring the directions given by a superior officer in the midst of
war. Instead of carrying out a quick-and-easy amputation, he saved
both a man's finger and his vocation, an action that placed human
needs first, for, in the words of Jesus, "the Sabbath is for man, not
man for the Sabbath" (Mark 2:27).

Later in life, having become a monk and then being ordained a
priest and bishop, Metropolitan Anthony would occasionally say,
"We should try to live in such a way that if the Gospels were lost,
they could be re-written by looking at us."[4]

3. Metropolitan Anthony of Sourozh, *The Essence of Prayer* (London: Darton,
Longman & Todd, 1986), xvi.

4. A personal memoir of Metropolitan Anthony of Sourozh: http://jimand
nancyforest.com/2008/02/metropolitan-anthony/.

Turning the Other Cheek

AT TIMES VIOLENCE can be an almost irresistible temptation. When I was in my early months in the U.S. Navy, being trained in meteorology at the Navy Weather School, someone in my unit borrowed a dollar from me but, despite my occasional requests, never got around to paying it back. He had the job of distributing the mail every day, a chore with an ounce of power among people starved for letters from home. Wearing his role as if it were a crown, he was not above delaying delivery of a letter addressed to anyone who annoyed him. Little by little everyone in our unit came to regard him with loathing.

One morning I demanded the return of my dollar. He looked at me with contempt, reached into his shirt pocket, took out a dollar bill, held it in front of my face, then let it fall to the floor.

Leaving the money where it fell, I grabbed him under the arms, lifted him off the floor, and hurled him against the wall. It still amazes me to remember how light he felt, how easily I made his body fly across the room. He came back with his fists flying. Far from being alarmed, I rejoiced in the combat, hammered away, hardly aware of the crowd that quickly gathered around us. The fight might well have lasted until I had done him some real harm—luckily a bell summoned us to inspection. As we stood at attention outside the barracks, I remember taking great pride in his bloodied lip and bruised face. Fortunately, when the inspecting officer asked him what had happened to his face, he told the prescribed lie—he had tripped on the stairs.

This battle won me a good deal of admiration at the time. I was immensely pleased with myself. It was as if I had successfully passed a manhood test. Even today the fight remains a shiny memory, though I was astonished—also alarmed—to discover what strength and deadly will I possessed when my anger was sufficiently aroused, and the exhilaration that battle can arouse.

Quite possibly that fight had something to do with the particular attention I later gave, when my conversion to Christianity began, to what the New Testament has to say about violence—for example: "Put away your sword, for those who live by the sword will perish by the sword" (Matthew 26:52). One could also say, "Put away your fists. Put away your will to harm or kill another human being." Two years later, while stationed with a Navy unit at the U.S. Weather Bureau just outside Washington, DC, I became a conscientious objector and, partly thanks to the backing I received from a senior officer in my command, was granted an early discharge.

One of the many texts that led me away from a military career was a passage in the Sermon on the Mount in which Jesus says, "If someone strikes you on the cheek, offer him the other also" (Matthew 5:39; Luke 6:23).

How different this is from the usual advice! So often the message is: If you are hit, hit back. Let your blow be harder than the one you received. In fact, you need not be hit at all in order to strike others. Provocation or the expectation of attack is warrant enough. Consider what vast numbers of people died or were gravely injured because of America's war with Iraq, an event justified on the suspicion, eventually shown to be without foundation, that Iraq possessed weapons of mass destruction.

"Turning the other cheek" is often seen as an especially suspect Christian doctrine. Many would say it is Jesus at his most unrealistic: "Human beings just aren't made that way." Some see turning the other cheek as promoting an ethic of self-abasement that borders on masochism. For men, the problem can be put even more simply: turning the other cheek isn't manly.

In fact turning the other cheek, in the sense Jesus intends and exemplifies, is quite manly, quite human, and very sensible.

One of the bravest men I have known was Jean Goss, a French soldier during World War II. Before his conversion to Christianity and a nonviolent way of life, Jean had been a deadly warrior. Following France's surrender to Germany, Jean spent four years in prison camps. He sometimes told this story from his days as a captive:

When Jesus was being beaten by the Roman soldiers, he wasn't silent. He said to his torturers: "Why do you strike me?" He could have kept quiet, because if you speak, you run the risk of another blow, or worse. Only the strongest are capable of turning the other cheek—but it can stop a massacre. It goes even further: it doesn't allow the other fellow to call himself a brute. I remember one of our guards in Germany. He had come back from the Russian front and sometimes had fits of raving madness. He would get carried away and start beating prisoners. One of them had the courage to go up to him and say, "I'm volunteering. If you need to brutalize someone, hit me." The torturer couldn't believe his ears. "How many blows do you want?" "I leave that to your conscience," answered the prisoner. That was the last straw, the thing you couldn't say: conscience. "I'm a brute, a tool, I'm not a conscience. I have no conscience. I haven't got the right to have a conscience." It took him some time to realize the opposite, that he had a conscience, but the flogging stopped.[1]

In 1975 something similar happened to Jean's wife, Hildegard Goss-Mayr, when she and the Argentinean human-rights activist Adolfo Perez Esquivel[2] were arrested in Brazil. In prison, the guards blindfolded them and made them listen to amplified recordings of prisoners being tortured. This went on for two days and might have led finally to their own torture, had not the Archbishop of São Paulo, Cardinal Arns, succeeded in convincing the military authorities to release them. Before being freed, the guards were ordered to feed them first, but Hildegard and Adolfo refused food. They said they wanted to fast because they acknowledged that they themselves, just like their guards, were co-responsible for the injustice in the world. They wanted to fast to free themselves from all the resentment toward these same guards and allow the guards' consciences to open up.

Often a person is hit because he is in the way. The blow is punishment for being there, and a warning to move on immediately or

---

1. Gerard Houver, *A Nonviolent Lifestyle: Conversations with Jean and Hildegard Goss-Mayr* (London: Lamp Books, Marshall Morgan & Scott, 1989), 3.

2. In 1980 Adolfo Perez Esquivel, co-founder of Servicio Paz y Justicia, was awarded the Nobel Prize for Peace.

more brutal consequences will follow. To turn the other cheek is not to give in and get out of the way; even at the risk of receiving another blow, you stay where you are but at the same time you refuse to respond with violence. Of course, there is always a risk in standing in the way of violent people—a nonviolent response does not guarantee one's safety any more than does a violent response. But there are times when one's faith and conscience lead one to risk even life itself. Consider one incident of collective "cheek turning" by devout Jews in Judaea in AD 26, just a few years before Jesus' execution. Half a century later, about AD 75, Flavius Josephus wrote this account:

> *The Jews rose up against Pilate in Caesarea to ask him to take the statues [of the emperor, regarded by the Jews as idols] away from Jerusalem. . . . When Pilate refused, they encamped around his house for five days and five nights. On the sixth day Pilate went before his tribunal in the great stadium and called the Jews together under the pretext of wanting to respond to their wishes. Then he gave armed soldiers the command to encircle the Jews. When the Jews saw how they were surrounded . . . they remained silent. Pilate, after declaring that he would have them killed if they would not honor the image of the emperor, gave the soldiers the sign to draw their swords. But the Jews threw themselves on the ground as if at a single command and offered their necks, all prepared to die rather than to violate God's law. Overcome by their religious zeal, Pilate gave the command to have the statues removed from Jerusalem.*[3]

A somewhat equivalent protest, in this case arousing the wrath of a Byzantine monarch, occurred in Constantinople in AD 815 when Emperor Leo V ordered the destruction of icons in churches, monasteries, and homes. It was his theory that the veneration of icons had been to blame for his recent military defeats—God had instead favored the iconoclast Muslims. For refusing to give in to Leo, the Patriarch of Constantinople, Nicephorus, was deposed and placed under house arrest. Possibly the most dramatic act of resistance that followed was an icon-bearing procession of a thousand monks

---

3. Flavius Josephus, *The Jewish War* 2.16.4.

led by the most respected abbot of the capital city, Saint Theodore the Studite,[4] who afterward paid for his stand with a flogging that nearly killed him followed by years of exile. Saint Theodore wrote to Emperor Leo, "Leave the Church to its pastors and masters. . . . If you refuse to do this and are bent on destroying our faith, know that though an angel came from heaven itself to pervert us we would not obey him. Far less would we obey you."[5] Finally, in 842, imperial objections to icons ended. The following year a church council confirmed the place of the icon in Christian life. (Ever since, the first Sunday of Great Lent has been set aside in Orthodox churches to celebrate the "Triumph of Orthodoxy." It is customary on that Sunday for the faithful to bring one of their home icons to the church.)

But we need not look far back in time for examples of brave men and women standing their ground while turning the other cheek, risking not only injury but their lives in order to "be obedient to God rather than man" (Acts 5:29).

In 1866, the American writer Henry David Thoreau coined the descriptive phrase "civil disobedience." Thoreau had gone to jail rather than pay a tax in support of the Mexican-American War. Ralph Waldo Emerson came to visit Thoreau in his cell. "Henry," Emerson asked, "what are you doing in there?" Thoreau replied, "Waldo, the question is what are you doing out there?" Thoreau raises a basic question: Is there not a place in the life of each person, when confronted with unjust laws and customs, for acts of civil disobedience? In his essay "Civil Disobedience" Thoreau explains his views:

> *Must the citizen ever for a moment, or in the least degree, resign his conscience to the legislator? Why has every man a conscience, then? I think that we should be men first, and subjects afterward. It is not desirable to cultivate a respect for the law, so much as for the*

---

4. Saint Theodore is also notable for his objection to slavery. His rule for monasteries included this command: "You shall possess no slave, neither for domestic service nor for the labor of the fields, for man is made in the image of God."

5. John Julian Norwich, *Byzantium: The Apogee* (London: Penguin Books, 1993), see chapter "The Return of Iconoclasm."

right. *The only obligation which I have a right to assume is to do at any time what I think right. It is truly enough said that a corporation has no conscience; but a corporation of conscientious men is a corporation with a conscience. Law never made men a whit more just; and, by means of their respect for it, even the well-disposed are daily made the agents of injustice.*[6]

Among the most classic defenses of civil disobedience is a letter addressed to local clergy written by Martin Luther King Jr. in 1963 while in jail in Birmingham, Alabama, for protesting racial segregation. Here is an extract:

One may well ask: "How can you advocate breaking some laws and obeying others?" The answer lies in the fact that there are two types of laws: just and unjust. I would be the first to advocate obeying just laws. One has not only a legal but a moral responsibility to obey just laws. Conversely, one has a moral responsibility to disobey unjust laws. I would agree with Saint Augustine that "an unjust law is no law at all."

Now, what is the difference between the two? How does one determine whether a law is just or unjust? A just law is a man-made code that squares with the moral law or the law of God. An unjust law is a code that is out of harmony with the moral law. To put it in the terms of Saint Thomas Aquinas: An unjust law is a human law that is not rooted in eternal law and natural law. Any law that uplifts human personality is just. Any law that degrades human personality is unjust. All segregation statutes are unjust because segregation distorts the soul and damages the personality. . . .

In no sense do I advocate evading or defying the law. . . . That would lead to anarchy. One who breaks an unjust law must do so openly, lovingly, and with a willingness to accept the penalty. I submit that an individual who breaks a law that conscience tells him is unjust, and who willingly accepts the penalty of imprisonment in

---

6. For the full text of the essay, "Civil Disobedience," see http://thoreau.eserver.org/civil.html.

order to arouse the conscience of the community over its injustice, is
in reality expressing the highest respect for law.[7]

There are countless examples of nonviolent civil disobedience
in recent times. Some of the most remarkable have to do with the
struggle against racism in the United States. Think of the many thousands who stood peacefully in the way of those who were intent on
maintaining racist divisions. Turning the other cheek, they received
many blows, stood ready to receive more, but refused to strike back.
Some died, many were injured, some were maimed for life, thousands were imprisoned, but from their brave nonviolent struggle
white Americans and many others began to recognize racism as a
grave sin and repent of it. Many laws were changed for the better. At
the same time, Christians everywhere developed a more profound
understanding of discipleship.

A determined woman named Rosa Parks played a major role in
awakening the American civil rights movement. Had it not been for
her, perhaps the name Martin Luther King would not have become
legendary. In the city of Montgomery, Alabama, Rosa Parks was
active in a local black church and had been the local secretary of the
National Association for the Advancement of Colored People. In
1955 she was working as a seamstress in a Montgomery department
store. On December 1, at the end of her working day and after doing
her shopping, she boarded a public bus:

> When I got on the bus, I noticed the bus driver [was the man who
> had once] evicted me from the bus because I had refused to pay my
> fare in the front and then get out and go around to the back to get
> in. Sometimes you would pay your fare, get out, start walking to the
> back of the bus, and then it would pull away before you got back in.
> They just left you behind!
>
> By the time I got on, the Negro section in the back of the bus was
> filled. But there was one vacant seat in the middle section, the part
> we could use as long as no white people wanted the seats. . . .

---

7. Martin Luther King Jr., "Letter from a Birmingham Jail," in *I Have a Dream:*
Writings and Speeches (New York: HarperOne, 2003), 83-100.

Rosa Parks, with
Martin Luther King Jr.
in the background

On the third stop a few white people boarded the bus and they took all the designated white seats. There was one white man left standing. The driver turned around and said he needed those front seats so this white man could take a seat, which meant the ones we [four black people] were sitting in. The four of us would have to stand up in order to accommodate this one white passenger. This was segregation.

When the driver first spoke, none of us moved. But then he spoke a second time with what I call a threat. He said, "You all better make it light on yourselves and let me have those seats." At that point the other three stood up. . . .

The driver looked at me and asked me if I was going to stand up. I told him no, I wasn't. He said, "If you don't stand up, I'm going to have you arrested." I told him to go on and have me arrested. I was too tired to stand. I didn't exchange any more words with him.

Rosa Parks was arrested, taken to the police station, her things taken away, and she was locked in a cell. She requested a drink of water but it was denied; the drinking fountain was for whites only.

"I wasn't happy at all," she remembers, "but I don't recall being extremely frightened. I just felt very much annoyed and inconvenienced because I had hoped to go home and cook supper and do whatever I had to do for the evening. But now I was sitting in jail and couldn't get home."[8]

That night a black lawyer, E. D. Nixon, bailed her out and promised he would defend her in court. Nixon phoned the ministers of the black churches in Montgomery and told them what had happened. That same evening forty clergymen, among them the young Martin Luther King Jr., a new pastor in town, met together and decided the time was right to try to end segregation of Montgomery's public transportation system. They agreed to begin a black boycott of the buses. King was elected to head the boycott, partly because, being the youngest, he had the least to lose should the campaign fail.

Several days after Rosa Park's arrest, a city judge found her guilty and ordered her to pay a $14 fine plus court costs. In the course of a year of prayer and protest that followed, the black population of Montgomery walked many thousands of miles without boarding a bus, enduring threats, abuse, and violence. Many were jailed, and the home of the King family bombed.

A year after Rosa Parks's refusal to give up her bus seat, the Supreme Court overturned her conviction, ruling that racial segregation in public transportation violated the U.S. Constitution. It was a major blow to segregation everywhere in the United States. December 21, 1956, was a historic day. Martin Luther King, a white minister at his side, and Rosa Parks rode together on Alabama's first integrated public bus.

"We will match your capacity to inflict suffering," said Dr. King, "with our capacity to endure suffering. We will meet your physical force with soul force. We will not hate you, but we cannot in good conscience obey your unjust laws . . . and in winning our freedom, we will win you in the process."[9]

---

8. *Martin Luther King: A Documentary*, ed. Flip Schulke (New York: Norton, 1976).

9. Martin Luther King Jr., "Stride toward Freedom," in Martin Luther King Jr., *A Testament of Hope* (New York: Harper & Row, 1986).

Forgiveness

*Forgiveness is the fragrance the violet sheds
on the heel that has crushed it.*
— Mark Twain

How dare we hope for God's mercy if we ourselves refuse to be merciful? How can we love someone whom we refuse to forgive? It's not possible. Love of enemies and the willingness to forgive are bound together. The insistence on forgiveness is a basic element of Christ's teaching.

The Greek verb used in the Our Father for "forgive," *aphiēmi*, means simply to let go, set aside, or leave behind. The verb, understood in its Greek sense, reminds us that forgiveness is, like love, not a feeling but an action involving our will rather than our emotions. But such a letting go never comes easy, not even for so great a saint as the apostle Peter. On one occasion he put the question to Jesus, "Lord, how many times must I forgive my brother or sister who has sinned against me?" Surely, Peter seems to be saying, there must be a limit. He asks if seven times would not be enough? Jesus answered, "I tell you, not seven times, but seventy times seven" (Matthew 18:21-22).

One of the desert saints of the early church, Abbot Moses the Black, found a dramatic way of proclaiming this Gospel principle. He was once asked to take part in a community meeting at which a certain lax brother was to be condemned and perhaps expelled from the brotherhood, but Abbot Moses was reluctant to attend. When he at last arrived, he was carrying a tattered reed basket on his back from which sand was pouring through many openings. "Why are you doing that?" he was asked. "My sins are running out behind, and

I do not see them, and today I come to judge the sins of another!"
The embarrassed community was moved to pardon their brother.[1]

As Saint Moses' simple action bore witness, nothing is more
fundamental to Jesus' teaching than his call to forgiveness and
mercy: giving up debts, letting go of grievances, pardoning those
who have harmed us. It's an element in the one prayer Jesus taught
his disciples. Every time we say the Lord's Prayer, we remind God
that we ask to be forgiven only insofar as we ourselves have extended
forgiveness to others: "And forgive us our trespasses as we forgive
those who trespass against us" (Matthew 6:12; Luke 11:2-4).

A few verses later in Matthew's Gospel, Jesus' teaching on this
point continues: "Judge not, that you be not judged. For with the
judgment you pronounce you will be judged, and the measure you
give will be the measure you get. Why do you see the speck that is
in your brother's eye, but fail to notice the log that is in your own?"
(Matthew 7:1-3).

This lesson is at the heart of Jesus' parable of the servant whose
king forgave him a huge debt, but who afterward refused to forgive
the small debt owed to him from a lesser servant and had the man
imprisoned. The outraged king says to the unforgiving man: "You
wicked servant! I forgave you all that debt because you besought me.
Should you not have mercy on your fellow servant as I had mercy on
you?" (Matthew 18:32-33).

It's not hard to identify with the reprimanded servant. Who
doesn't know how much easier it is to ask God to forgive us than to
extend forgiveness to others?

In the eucharistic liturgy of the Orthodox Church, the most
frequent response to the many petitions included in the litanies is
"Lord have mercy." This appeal for God's forgiveness is repeated
countless times at every service.[2]

1. Thomas Merton, *The Wisdom of the Desert* (New York: New Directions, 1960), 40.

2. An English translation of the full text of the Liturgy of Saint John Chrysostom is available at http://orthodoxengland.org.uk/dlosjc.htm.

I know few people for whom forgiveness—being merciful—isn't a day-by-day challenge. We have been wounded, and the wounds often last a lifetime and even spill across generations. As children, as parents, as husbands or wives, as families, as workers, as jobless people, as church members, as members of certain classes or races, as voters, as citizens of particular nations, we have been violated, targeted, lied to, used, abandoned. Sins, often serious sins, have been committed against us. We may feel damaged, scarred for life, stunted. People we love—children, spouses, friends—may even have died of evil done to them. In my own family I often think of my stepmother, Karla, shot dead as she stood waiting for a bus in San Francisco. Every family has its tragic stories.

But we are not only victims with just cause to be angry. In various ways we are linked to injuries others have suffered and are still suffering. If I allow myself to see how far the ripples extend from my small life, I will discover that not only in the places I inhabit and work but on the far side of the planet there are people who are among my victims. Through what I have done or failed to do, through what my community has done or failed to do, there are others whose lives are more wretched than they might have been. The inexpensive shirt I bought—or blouse you bought—may have been made by a woman laboring for meager pay in a firetrap in Pakistan.

We feel justified in condemning the evils we see in others while excusing and justifying the evils we're responsible for ourselves; our own sins, it seems, are much more defensible than theirs. In the area of enmity, we fail to realize that those who threaten us feel threatened by us, and often have good reasons for their fears.

Enmity is often rooted in the unwillingness to forgive.

The problem is not simply a personal issue, for the greatest sins of enmity are committed *en masse* with very few people feeling any personal responsibility for the violence or destruction they share in doing or preparing. "I was only following orders" is one of humanity's most frequently repeated justifications for killing, heard as often from those who profess religious convictions as from those who deny them.

My friend Hildegard Goss-Mayr tells a remarkable story of a step toward forgiveness that occurred in Poland ten years after the end of World War II. By then the division of Europe had become iron-hard, a nuclear arms race was underway, and the Cold War was getting colder by the day. In Warsaw to take part in a conference, she and her husband, Jean Goss, met privately one evening with a group of Poles to discuss the Stalinist regime that had been imposed on their country, the possibilities for giving nonviolent witness together whenever human rights were violated, and the possibility of collaboration in peacemaking between Poles and Germans:

Defying a law prohibiting group meetings, we met in a flat with some twenty young intellectuals, all committed Christians. It was their first opportunity to meet Christians from the West. The exchange was profound and sincere. It was already late when Jean and I decided to ask a question that was very much on the minds of many young West Germans we knew. . . . "Would you be willing," we asked, "if the possibility should arise, to meet with Christians from West Germany? They want to ask forgiveness for what Germany did to Poland during the war and to begin to build a new relationship." There was a silence. Finally one of our Polish friends, a young writer, jumped up and vehemently said, "Jean and Hildegard, we love you, you are our friends but what you are asking is impossible! Each stone of Warsaw has been soaked in Polish blood. We cannot forgive!"

We tried to insist: "Who should make the first step? The non-believers? The Communists? Someone else? Or we who are baptized in the name of the One who pardoned the sin of all humanity and overcame hatred through the gift of his life?" But our Polish friend said this was impossible. "This is not yet the time for forgiveness."

Even after a decade, the war wounds remained fresh and deep. Jean and I saw we could go no further. It was getting late. Before separating, we proposed that we recite together the prayer that unites us all, the Our Father. All joined in willingly. But when we got to the passage, "and forgive us our sins as we forgive . . . ," our Polish friends halted in the prayer.

Into this silence the one who had said, "it is impossible," spoke up in a low voice: "I must say yes to you. I could no more pray the Our Father, I could no longer call myself a Christian, if I refuse to forgive. Humanly speaking, I cannot do it, but God will give us his strength!"

It was at that point that all of us understood that peacemaking is impossible without conversion of the heart.

We continued to talk and plan. A year-and-a-half later, after more moderate leaders had replaced the Stalinists, ten of our Polish friends who had been in that room were given visas that allowed them to take part in a meeting in Vienna, the first East–West [International Fellowship of Reconciliation] conference after the war, and here they met with the Germans. From this meeting, many initiatives in East–West relations began. The friendships and consequences continue until today.[3]

Think of this story the next time you recite the Our Father.

We often hear the phrase "forgive and forget." But must true forgiveness imply a willingness to forget? Clearly there is no benefit in hanging on to the memory of trivial events. It's good advice to forget them. But there are events that it would be a sin to forget. As the Orthodox theologian and scholar Metropolitan Kallistos Ware has written,

It would not be right to say to the members of the Armenian nation, "Forget the massacres of 1915," or to the Jewish people, "Forget the Shoah in the Second World War." These are matters that, for the sake of our shared humanity, none of us should forget, not least so as to ensure that such atrocities may never be allowed to happen again. . . . Remember the past but do not be held captive by it. Turn

3. Hildegard Goss-Mayr, "An Experience of Forgiveness in Poland," published in the April 1986 issue of *Reconciliation International*, journal of the International Fellowship of Reconciliation.

*it into a blessing, not a curse; a source of hope, not humiliation.
Our memories are not to be repressed or negated, but at the same
time they require to be purified and healed. We need to remember
. . . in a spirit of compunction and mourning. We need to remember
with love. . . . Forgiveness is not primarily our human action but a
divine action in which we humans participate.*[4]

Yes, I am sometimes reminded, forgiveness is a wonderful thing.
But what about anger? Haven't I a right to my anger? When I am
hurt, should I pretend not to feel the hurt? And if I manage to hide
my hurt and anger, am I not lying?

How easy it is to become an anger-centered, anger-driven person,
but it's a condition that solves no problems and makes many worse.
Saint Gregory of Nyssa, one of the most revered theologians of the
early church, saw the anger that lies behind the refusal of forgiveness
as self-destructive: "In condemning your neighbor, you thereby condemn yourself."[5] In a similar vein, the American writer Mark Twain
remarked, "Anger is an acid that can do more harm to the vessel in
which it is stored than to anything on which it is poured." A com-
parable insight is attributed to the Buddha: "Anger, like a forest fire,
burns up its own support."

Anger and fear are often intertwined—anger a suit of armor in
which fear is hidden. Anger has its place, but it's best if it resembles
the brief flame topping a matchstick rather than a permanent volcanic inferno. We see anger in Jesus' life but only in brief flashes. He
was furious with those who made a house of worship into a place of
thieves; he denounced those who laid on others heavy burdens they
did not carry themselves. If you want to see Jesus angry, read the
twenty-third chapter of Matthew's Gospel.

Yes, anger can have its place, while a forgiveness that is pretended,
that attempts to hide pain and rage behind pretty wallpaper, is of no
value. Sooner or later we will discover that our complaints are still

4. Kallistos Ware: "Forgive Us as We Forgive," http://www.incommunion.
org/2013/10/01/kallistos-forgiveness/.

5. Gregory of Nyssa, *The Lord's Prayer, The Beatitudes*, homily 5, ed. Hilda
Graef (New York: Newman Press, 1954), 73.

there, still fresh, perhaps more explosive than ever. Until we allow ourselves to feel the hurt and to express it, it is unlikely that a genuine act of forgiveness will be possible.

If the pardon we seek to offer to those who need our forgiveness is to be of any use to them, they need to be aware of what they have done and the pain or hurt it has caused. How can they know it if we are silent? Jesus teaches that we have the obligation to speak out: "Take heed to yourselves; if your brother sins, rebuke him, and if he repents, forgive him" (Luke 17:3). Where sincere regret is lacking, one's forgiveness of the other is incomplete—freeing for oneself but shrugged off by the other.

A flash of anger—the sort of anger that the Jesuit poet Daniel Berrigan describes as "outraged love"—may help the other person to realize the gravity of the sin he or she has committed and open the path toward forgiveness. But until we have allowed ourselves to get beyond anger, to forgive, or rather to let God's forgiveness flow through us, we are burdened with our injuries and complaints every bit as much as the ghost of Jacob Marley was held captive by chains and money boxes in Charles Dickens's *Christmas Carol*.

We are called to forgive. We need to seek forgiveness, offer forgiveness, and accept forgiveness. We are followers of Jesus who taught us forgiveness even when his hands were nailed to the wood of the cross: "Father, forgive them. They know not what they do" (Luke 23:34).

Breaking Down the Dividing Wall of Enmity

SAINT PAUL MAKES an extraordinary claim: in Christ enmity is destroyed. He wrote this declaration in a letter sent to the recently founded church in Ephesus:

> *For Christ is our peace, who has made us both one and has broken down the dividing wall of enmity . . . that he might create in himself one new person in place of two, so making peace, and might reconcile us both to God in one body through the cross, thereby bringing enmity to an end.* (Ephesians 2:14-16)

Walls would have been on Paul's mind at the time; in the same letter he mentions that he is "a prisoner for the Lord." His guidance was sent from within prison walls.

There is a similar passage in Paul's letter to the Christian community in Galatia, where apparently the local church was being torn apart by all sorts of division. Among those who have been baptized, Paul insisted, there could only be profound unity:

> *There is neither Jew nor Greek, there is neither slave nor free, there is neither male nor female; for you are all one in Christ Jesus.* (Galatians 3:28)

If even within the newborn church rifts were a serious problem, how much worse was conflict in the surrounding culture. The *Pax Romana* was maintained not by peaceful means but by the emperor's legions. Death by violence was a common event. Public entertainment in those times included games in which the losers were killed. Few gladiators died of old age.

In the immediate context of Jesus' activities in Galilee and Judea, "the dividing wall of enmity" stood massively between Jews and Romans. Friendly social contact between them would have been rare. But one day a centurion, a senior officer of the Roman army, appealed to Jesus for help:

> *The centurion had a slave who was dear to him, who was sick and at the point of death. When he heard of Jesus, he sent to him elders of the Jews, asking him to come and heal his slave. And when they came to Jesus, they besought him earnestly, saying, "He is worthy to have you do this for him, for he loves our nation, and he built us our synagogue." And Jesus went with them. When he was not far from the house, the centurion sent friends to him, saying, "Lord, do not trouble yourself, for I am not worthy to have you come under my roof . . . but say the word and let my servant be healed.". . . When Jesus heard this he marveled at him. . . . And when those who had been sent returned to the house, they found the slave well.* (Luke 7:1-10)

Witnessing Jesus respond positively to the petition of a Roman soldier must have been a bitter pill to swallow for his nationalist-minded disciples, and still more galling for them to hear Jesus remark afterwards, "I tell you, not even in Israel have I found such faith."

Matthew reports that Jesus "marveled" at the faith of the centurion, who saw no need for Jesus to be physically present to heal someone. The centurion explained that he is used to governing others: "I say to one, 'Go,' and he goes." (In Roman law soldiers of any rank had the right to demand that anyone they met on the road carry their equipment for one Roman mile; thus was Simon of Cyrene conscripted to carry the cross when Jesus no longer had the strength to do so. Jesus was referring to this law when he said that his followers should volunteer to go a second mile freely [Matthew 5:41]—doing more than is required or expected had the potential of opening a door in the dividing wall of enmity.)

Jesus had another reason to be astonished: here was a Roman making a *request* rather than issuing a command, a Roman who respected Jews! Assuming that Jesus might not believe something so unlikely, the centurion had sent ahead Jewish elders to bear witness to Jesus that this Roman loved the Jewish nation and had even contributed money to build a synagogue. The centurion's attitude toward Jesus was that of a recruit standing before a general.

It is a remarkable story: a Roman reaching out to a Jew, a professional soldier to a man who has chosen to be disarmed, the two brought together by a dying slave held dear by the centurion. In their encounter, the dividing wall of enmity collapsed.

Walls. We live in a world of walls. Competition, contempt, repression, racism, nationalism, violence, and domination: these are seen as normal and sane. Enmity is normal. Self and self-interest, narrowly defined, form the center point of many lives, while love and the refusal to center one's own life on enmity, to reach out compassionately to an adversary, are likely to be dismissed as naïve, idealistic, even unpatriotic or traitorous.

Behind walls lie weapons. In at least seven countries, at every hour of the day, missiles armed with nuclear warheads stand ready for launch. So far only two such weapons have been used in war—in two blinding flashes Hiroshima and Nagasaki were destroyed in 1945—but there have been many close calls and accidents[1] plus hundreds of test explosions, with even these, when done in the open air, causing many deaths by cancer for those downwind.

Other weapons of mass destruction, both chemical and biological, also exist. A list of "conventional" weapons in actual rather than potential use would, if briefly described in small type, fill a sizable book. Hour by hour, people are being killed in war or perishing of its side effects. How many per day? God knows—those who do the killing prefer not to know. The number is not small. The typical victims are the most vulnerable—children, the aged, the ill—while those in command are the least likely to die. Then there is the further cost in suffering and death because the money spent on weapons is

---

1. For a detailed account of nuclear catastrophes that almost happened, see Eric Schlosser, *Command and Control: Nuclear Weapons, the Damascus Accident, and the Illusion of Safety* (New York: Penguin Press, 2013).

not available for health care and other desperate human and environmental needs.

We live in dread of the weapons of our enemies, and they of ours. We are quite prepared to do much worse to them—and they to us—than take an eye for an eye. The regime-change war in Iraq is among recent examples of "preemptive" attack. The cost is phenomenal, not only financially but in terms of the millions of people busy every day in war planning and weapons manufacture.

There are also less tangible costs—both spiritual and psychological. How many of us live in a state of "low-grade" depression that is rooted in work and habits of thought that have death at its core? As every pharmacist knows from the sale of tranquilizers and sleep aids, depression is widespread. Grim expectations about the future are among the causes. Those who have taken part in war include many thousands who suffer from what in World War I was called battle fatigue or shell shock and today is called post-traumatic stress disorder (PTSD). Among U.S. veterans of recent wars, the suicide rate is high—more have died of self-inflicted violence than died in the war zones.

Yet setting the stage for another—perhaps a final—world war has its advocates. There are even those who see such a war as an enactment of God's will, the fulfillment of prophecies, the means whereby God will exercise judgment and cut the thread of history in a holocaust in which the ungodly will be consumed while the elect will be lifted rapturously into heaven. The grim theology behind such a conception of God could be summed up as "And God so loved the world that he sent World War III." Such a "god" has much in common with Stalin and Hitler, a sadistic deity reigning over ever-lasting gulags and concentration camps.

Whoever we are, whatever our opinions, whatever political party we side with and vote for, we are, through national structures if not personal conviction, participants in major structures of enmity and thus are called upon not to create openings in the dividing wall of enmity but to redouble the thickness of the wall.

Confronted with such deeply embedded hostility, how can anyone contribute to reconciliation even in small degrees?

Thomas Merton
photo: Jim Forest

The beginnings must take root in our spiritual lives. One of Thomas Merton's insights was the realization that reconciliation is not simply a formal coming together of people who have been divided, an event arranged by leaders. It is prefigured in our own spiritual lives. As Merton wrote,

> *If I can unite in myself the thought and devotion of Eastern and West-ern Christendom, the Greek and the Latin Fathers, the Russian and the Spanish mystics, I can prepare in myself the reunion of divided Christians. From that secret and unspoken unity in myself can even-tually come a visible and manifest unity of all Christians. If we want to bring together what is divided, we cannot do so by imposing one division upon the other. If we do this, the union is not Christian. It is political and doomed to further conflict. We must contain all the divided worlds in ourselves and transcend them in Christ.*[2]

---

2. Thomas Merton, *Conjectures of a Guilty Bystander* (New York: Doubleday, 1966), 12.

Merton's insight has to do not only with ending inter-Christian schism. To "contain the divided worlds in ourselves and transcend them in Christ" suggests that, no matter what objections we have to other cultures and political systems, we have to value and recognize as human those living within such systems. Yet, far from doing so, rarely do we even know them and rarer still are we able to speak even polite fragments of their language. (It isn't necessarily the same on both sides. When the Cold War was deeply frozen, there were more teachers of English in the Soviet Union than there were students of Russian in the United States and Britain combined.)

Though a chill remains, the Cold War is over. In its place we have the War on Terror. Dread and hostility of the Muslim world are pounded into us. Through films, novels, and news reports—daily helpings of the Gospel according to John Wayne—we are given vivid reminders of why enmity is essential.

News reports are often the hardest to guard against, for we tend to view the press as an independent and objective channel of communication, but even those newspapers and broadcasters that actually attempt genuine objectivity inevitably reflect national points of view. Enemy images are forged and reforged, images that give us no glimpse of what is human or decent in our adversaries, images that in the end condemn us to war.

In many ways the news media can be compared to a trash-collection agency. Our press collects stories about what is wrong in Country X—while our opposite numbers in Country X do the same to us. In the case of Al Qaeda, it becomes still more nebulous, because it's a transnational web of militant movements that see themselves as protecting their grim version of Islam. The information provided by the mass media is mainly true but radically incomplete. Whatever would animate understanding, sympathy, compassion, or a sense of identification is excluded.

To overcome the propaganda of enmity, we need to discover what Thomas Merton called "the human dimension." As he wrote in one of his letters to me,

The basic problem is not political, it is human. One of the most important things to do is to keep cutting deliberately through politi-

cal lines and barriers and emphasizing that these are largely fab-
rications and that there is a genuine reality, totally opposed to the
fictions of politics: the human dimension which politics pretends to
arrogate entirely to themselves.[3]

How does one enter the human dimension of a people living far
away, speaking a language we do not speak, whose lives, fears, and
cultures we experience through the smoky lens of the mass media?

There are ways . . .

If you can do it, one excellent way is to travel to places most
of your neighbors wouldn't dream of visiting. Even in the case of
countries at war or on the edge of war, there are groups promoting
person-to-person encounter.

In my own case, the most life-changing experiences of travel in
an enemy land occurred in the 1980s, the final decade of the Soviet
Union and a decade when World War III seemed far from unlikely.

During the late 1970s and early '80s, the Western peace movement chiefly focused on the danger posed by nuclear weapons and
the civilization-destroying consequences that would result from
their actual use. Almost no effort was made to develop programs of
face-to-face contact—the building of human bridges between East
and West. For most Americans and their European allies, Russians
were seen as a gray and godless people marching in lockstep. Nothing was being done to challenge the stereotype.

Neither side made East–West contact easy. In those tense days,
just getting a visa to Soviet Russia was a major achievement. The
authorities in Moscow were reluctant to permit entry to any visitor
who lacked a "pro-Soviet" outlook. In my case, as general secretary
of the International Fellowship of Reconciliation, a peace organization that was outspoken in its opposition to the war Soviet troops
were then fighting in Afghanistan, I and others from IFOR were
regarded as high-risk visitors. A Soviet journalist visiting Amster-

---

3. Thomas Merton, from a letter to Jim Forest, included in a collection of letters by Thomas Merton, *The Hidden Ground of Love*, ed. William Shannon (New
York: Farrar, Straus & Giroux, 1985), 272.

dam told me that there was worry in the Kremlin that our attempt at dialog in Moscow might only be a pretext for holding an antiwar demonstration in Red Square.

After about a year of effort, the visas we had sought were issued. This allowed our participation in a small but ground-breaking theological consultation hosted by the Russian Orthodox Church and co-sponsored by the International Fellowship of Reconciliation. My own visa allowed me to arrive in Russia several days before the rest of our group in order to help with preparations.

That week-long stay in Moscow was the occasion for my discovery of how much Cold War imagery was lodged in my own head. I became aware of this even as I stepped onto the aircraft. Although flying to Moscow was no more remarkable than flying to San Francisco, Rome, or Tokyo, it seemed that, in crossing the "Iron Curtain," I was on my way to another planet. In my imagination, I had stepped into the world of James Bond. Staff at the poorly lit airport at which our plane touched down, Sheremetyevo, fit the script. My face was repeatedly checked against my passport photo, the visa examined carefully to make sure it wasn't forged, and everything in my suitcase gone over with a fine-toothed comb.

Once inside my hotel room, I could all but see a KGB agent in an adjacent room listening to my rustling noises as I unpacked my suitcase. In my mind's eye the walls might as well have been made of glass. I looked around the room, curious where the microphone was hidden. Perhaps inside the ceiling lamp? (And probably the room *was* bugged. Secret police in every country do this kind of thing all the time. I remember in the early 1970s finding a micro-transmitter concealed in the office telephone of Emmaus House in New York City. Our community's intense involvement in the antiwar movement meant that we were watched closely by the F.B.I., and during one period in 1971 were under daily surveillance.)

But there were situations in Moscow where it was possible to see that the shaping of my expectations by the Cold War didn't entirely match reality. I love walking, and that first night, well past my usual bedtime, I was too awake to lie down, so I decided to go for a midnight walk down the wide avenue that led to the Kremlin and Red Square several miles to the east. The weather was damp, the streets glistening. Moscow in those days was a city with little nightlife— there were few cars and still fewer pedestrians. I recall glancing behind me, expecting to find a shadowy figure following me, another experience I had had on a number of occasions in the United States during the Vietnam War. Surely a dissident from the West who had much in common with Russian dissidents wouldn't be permitted to wander about unwatched. But that night no minders were to be seen. Reaching Red Square, I found the only others enduring the rain that had begun to fall were the two statue-like soldiers guarding Lenin's Tomb. It was the first of many nighttime excursions in Russia.

Within a few days I felt more at ease in my wanderings. Not yet having a footing in the Cyrillic alphabet, I often had to turn to strangers for help. Sooner or later I would find someone who could manage to understand me and would point me in the right direction. I came to feel especially secure in the Metro, the underground train system with its cathedral-like stations that dot central Moscow. Decorated with Stalin-era mosaics and sculptures, one station was as baroque as a concert hall in Mozart's day. But more interesting than the stations were the passengers. Apart from those in military uniform, few were wearing clothing that would stand out in either the London Underground or in New York subways. I recall one child staring at me with avid curiosity, perhaps because I have a beard, which was unusual in Soviet Russia. Her head was pressed against her father's chest as she sat on his lap, holding his hand in the same way my daughter Anne would have gripped mine back home in Holland.

And there were couples. Somehow I was surprised that Russians should be as demonstrably in love with each other as their Amsterdam or New York counterparts. In a particularly crowded Metro carriage during rush hour, I happened to be jammed against one pair whose heads were inclined toward each other so that their noses touched, yet they seemed as alone in the Metro as Romeo and Juliet in a Verona garden.

In those isolated times, with visitors from the West a rarity, Russians were fascinated by foreigners and were, contrary to everything I had been told, often approachable. In an especially complex Metro station, with several intersecting lines, two students eager to practice their English helped me from one Metro platform to another. They asked me if I liked the poetry of Robert Burns. Exaggerating a bit, I said I did. They recited some of his verses and before parting we sang, "Should old acquaintance be forgot . . ."

Looking back, it occurs to me that this book had its beginning in Moscow. It was in the course of conversations with strangers that I began to think afresh about Jesus' remarkable stress on love of enemies. If that's to happen, surely it happens best by meeting the people at whom our weapons are aimed. Part of the cure is the development of cross-border friendships. I thought of a sentence in another letter Merton had sent me: "In the end, it is the reality of personal relationships that saves everything."[4]

Thanks to the continuing hospitality of the Russian Orthodox Church, the first visit led to many more. In 1986, in the early months of the Gorbachev era, I was able to begin wide-ranging travels in the Soviet Union while researching a book, *Pilgrim to the Russian Church*, published two years later. Then came still more travel while I did the research for a second book, *Religion in the New Russia*. During these far-reaching journeys that brought me across six of Russia's eight time zones, it was my privilege to witness the end of Soviet persecution of religious life and also to observe at close range what proved to be the last few years of the Soviet Union.

East–West programs such as the one in which I was engaged contributed in a significant measure to ending the Cold War, a major historical event. That's the headline. But the back-page story was that my own life was also changed in unexpected ways. This was mainly due to the experiences I had in Russian churches.

My expectation of religious life in Russia, largely shaped by Western press reports, was that I would be visiting a church on its last legs— congregations mainly of old women whose ranks were steadily thin-

---

4. Letter to Jim Forest, February 21, 1966; published in *Hidden Ground of Love*, ed. Shannon, 294-97.

ning out as they died. Decades of intimidation by a militantly atheist
regime, a persecution in which millions perished and countless places
of worship were destroyed or put to other uses, must be paying off.
The church in Russia was surely on the edge of the grave.

Except it wasn't. Though "working churches" were few and far
between except in a few major cities, believers attending services
in churches that remained open were packed together like upright
matchsticks. Most, it's true, were populated mainly by older
women, some of whom looked like tractor drivers. They stood for
long services without batting an eye. (Following the tradition of
the early church, Orthodox churches in Russia have no pews, only
a few chairs and benches for those who need them. Russians pray
standing up.)

The climate of prayer in Russian Orthodox churches was as dense
as Russian black bread. If the walls and pillars were taken away, I felt
the roof would stay where it was, so intense was the engagement of
the laity with the priests and deacons serving at the altar. The sign of
the cross, often accompanied by a small bow, was frequently made
by each worshiper. Only in black churches in America had I sometimes experienced so deep an immersion in prayer or a similar integration of body and soul.

On one occasion I was in a Moscow church with a Lutheran
friend from Sweden, Margareta, who had never before made much
use of her body as an active partner in prayer. She stood still as a
statue until the much shorter Russian woman standing at her right
side took Margareta's hand and, as if teaching her granddaughter,
showed her how to make the sign of the cross. The *babushka* wanted
to make sure no one was passively standing around watching as if in
a museum. For the rest of the service Margareta crossed herself as
often as the *babushka* who had guided her hand, a woman who was a
typical representative of those people, chiefly women, who had carried the faith intact through the Stalin years. (Why mainly women?
One of them explained to me, "It's easier for us. The authorities don't
like punishing gray-haired ladies. They write us off as crazy. They are
harder on the men.")

At the invitation of a Russian bishop, Nancy was able to come

with me for a summer trip in 1987. Our shared experiences of worship in Russia renewed and reshaped spiritual life within our family.
Using the Litany of Peace from the Orthodox liturgy, we began to
pray together just before bedtime, standing before the several icons
that had found their way into our home. Finally, in 1988, we made
the frontier-crossing step of joining a Russian Orthodox parish in
Amsterdam. Since then our eucharistic life has been rooted in the
Orthodox Church, though we see ourselves as living on a bridge
that links East and West. Still feeling an intimate connection with
Catholicism, we draw courage from the words of Saint Philaret of
Moscow, who led the Russian Orthodox Church in the middle of
the nineteenth century: "The walls we build on earth do not reach
to heaven."[5]

While travel to enemy lands doesn't often have consequences
that so radically reorient one's life as was the case for Nancy and me,
certainly one sees the world differently and even lives differently.
One's native land is no longer the all-powerful center and its norms
no longer universal norms.

As helpful and even life changing as travel can sometimes be, a
passport and ticket to faraway places aren't the only way to go on
a pilgrimage of peacemaking. There are many things one can do to
break down enmity without boarding an aircraft or crossing a border.

One way to leap the world's walls without leaving home is to use
the Internet as a magic carpet. If you want to know more about a
country that is currently a target of war or in danger of becoming
one, there are numerous websites and blogs that will give you a more
three-dimensional perspective than you are likely to obtain via local
mass media. Of course, caution and discernment are needed, but
that's just as true with local news sources.

Better yet, there is the door of literature. Preparing for my trav-

---

5. Philaret's daring utterances brought him into imperial disfavor from 1845
until the accession of Tsar Alexander II a decade later. For a time, Philaret was
restricted to the limits of his diocese. He is said to have helped prepare Alexander II's proclamation freeing the serfs. He also made a major contribution to the
translation of the Bible from Church Slavonic, inaccessible to most people, into
Russian. Among Philaret's many correspondents was the poet Alexander Pushkin.

els in Russia, the best of all classrooms was provided by Russian authors, some prerevolutionary (Dostoevsky, Chekhov, Gogol, Tolstoy, Leskov); others, postrevolutionary (Mikhail Bulgakov, Boris Pasternak, Vladimir Soloukhin, Anna Akhmatova, Yevgeny Yevtushenko, and Aleksandr Solzhenitsyn). Each country has authors who can carry the reader into intimate spaces the guide-book-dependent traveler will never reach.

There is also the entrance point provided by films that may not be seen on TV or in local cinemas but can be found on DVD. One of the major inspirations for my travels in Russia was seeing *Moscow Does Not Believe in Tears,* a Soviet-made production that was honored with an Oscar in 1980. Starting in the late 1950s, the film follows the lives of three women who become friends while sharing a room in a Moscow dormitory. Their lives carry them in quite different directions, but the bond between them never breaks. Besides opening a nonpolitical window on Russian life in the Brezhnev era, the film also remains rewarding both as a love story and a social comedy.[6] Every nation has its own film industry, and today, thanks to the Web, it is much easier to find, rent, or buy captioned films from countries and cultures that we regard as actual or potential enemies.

One of the most enjoyable ways to break through the dividing wall of enmity is by sharing the table of those we are armed against. Get a cookbook of the cuisine of a particular country or region and find the right ingredients, even if substitutions may be needed. Invite friends for a home meal or make it a parish event. Include readings and music from the country whose food you are enjoying. Such "meals of reconciliation" not only make an unforgettable event but help form new attitudes.

Not least there are the threads of connection created by prayer. As aids to prayer I sometimes cut out newspaper and magazine photos that catch my eye and keep them in a Bible or prayer book. One does

---

6. I recently learned that U.S. president Ronald Reagan watched the film several times prior to his meetings with the president of the Soviet Union, Mikhail Gorbachev, in order to gain a better understanding of "the Russian soul."

not need to know names to pray for those in a photo. God knows them by name.

Taking such steps, the dividing wall of enmity breaks down brick by brick. Love of enemies not only becomes possible; it becomes difficult not to love them. Even when you discover things you find appalling about structures in which people in enemy countries are to some degree engaged, you can no longer think of them merely as things but as people bearing the image of God.

Beginning to know personally those who are the targets of war, praying for them daily, listening to their music, reading their literature, bringing their food to the table—these are truly disarming experiences. It becomes unthinkable to do anything that might result in their being shot or burned alive, for truly they are our sisters and brothers. We discover that their lives are in our care, and ours in theirs.

The dividing wall of enmity runs, of course, not just between nations or between soldiers in opposing armies but between individuals near at hand—a spouse, a teenage child, a relative, a neighbor, a colleague, people of differing religious convictions and faiths, people at odds with one another in parishes, people of opposing political parties, and often includes politicians and national political leaders.

It would require a much larger book than this one to explore all the varieties of conflict and to look at models of conflict resolution and healing—the removal of the dividing wall of enmity. But in every case prayer for the other, prayer for forgiveness and reconciliation provides a starting point. Reconciliation begins with wanting it to happen, glimpsing its benefits, and realizing that changes in relationship patterns require not only change in the other but change in me.

Refusing to Take an Eye for an Eye

In the Sermon on the Mount, Jesus calls on his listeners to renounce retaliation and vengeance:

> You have heard that it was said, "An eye for an eye and a tooth for a tooth." But I say to you, do not resist the one who is evil. (Matthew 5:38-39)

One of the remarkable features of Christianity is that its founder healed many and killed no one, setting an example of a life free of eye-for-an-eye vengeance. He refused to sanction acts of violence no matter how justifiable by ordinary human standards. In rescuing from execution a woman caught in adultery, he sentenced to death the death sentence, saying, "Has no one condemned you? Neither do I condemn you. Go and sin no more" (John 7:53-8:11). When Peter used violence to defend Jesus, he was instantly admonished: "Put away your sword, for whoever lives by the sword will perish by the sword" (Matthew 26:52). Jesus' last healing miracle before the Resurrection was done to an enemy who was among those who came to arrest him in the Garden of Gethsemane, the man wounded by Peter's sword, a servant of the high priest: "Jesus admonished his disciples, 'No more of this!' Then he touched the wounded man's ear and it was healed" (Luke 22:51).

But how are we to understand the verse's second sentence: "But I say to you do not resist the one who is evil"? While we see Jesus giving an example of nonresistance during the hours that led up to his crucifixion, are we obliged to be passive in the face of evil? Is every form of resistance banned? Not at all. Here "not to resist" means not to replicate the injustice or violence of the adversary, not to become your adversaries' mirror image. It's the rejection of the blow-counter-blow cycle: you hit me, I hit you, you hit me back again, until one or both of us is knocked out or dead.

Christ's rejection of retribution is the flip side of living a life that connects us to the Kingdom of God—the paschal kingdom in which life is not shaped by violence and death. As Saint John Chrysostom wrote in the fourth century, "We resist evil by surrendering ourselves to suffer wrongfully. In this way you shall prevail over the evil one. For one fire is not quenched by another, but fire by water."[1]

From the first century until today, Christians have been resisting evil while refusing to use evil means. For several hundred years after the Resurrection, the followers of Jesus were renowned—or infamous—for their refusal to worship the traditional gods or to regard the ruler as a deity and also for their refusal to perform military service, or, for those converted while in the army, for refusing to kill. As Saint Justin Martyr wrote in the second century,

> We who were filled with war and mutual slaughter and every wickedness have each of us in all the world changed our weapons of war . . . swords into plows and spears into pruning hooks.[2] . . . We who formerly murdered one another now not only do not make war upon our enemies but, that we may not lie or deceive our judges, we gladly die confessing Christ.[3]

In the same century, Clement of Alexandria described the church as "an army that sheds no blood." In Pauline terms, he describes the spiritual warfare in which Christians participate:

> Now the trumpet sounds with a mighty voice calling the soldiers of the world to arms, announcing war. And shall not Christ, who has uttered his summons to peace even to the ends of the earth, summon together his own soldiers of peace? Indeed, O Man, he has called to arms with his Blood and his Word an army that sheds no blood. To

---

1. John Chrysostom, Homily on the Gospel of Matthew 18.1, using the translation found in *The Ancient Christian Commentary on Scripture, Matthew 1-13* (Chicago: InterVarsity Press, 2001), 118.

2. Justin Martyr, *Dialogue with Trypho* 110.

3. Justin Martyr, *1 Apology* 39.

these soldiers he has handed over the Kingdom of Heaven. . . . Let us be armed for peace, putting on the armor of justice, seizing the shield of salvation, and sharpening the "sword of the spirit which is the Word of God." (Ephesians 6:13-17)

This is how the Apostle [Paul] prepares us for battle. Such are the arms that make us invulnerable. So armed, let us prepare to fight the Evil One. Let us cut through his flaming attack with the blade which the Logos Himself has tempered in the waters of Baptism. Let us reply to His goodness by praise and thanksgiving. Let us honor God with His divine Word: "While thou art yet speaking," He says, "Here I am."[4]

In the *Canons* of Hippolytus, attributed to Hippolytus, a bishop of Rome in the late second century,[5] one finds a section that concentrates on the baptism of soldiers and judges:

Concerning the magistrate and the soldier: they are not to kill anyone, even if they receive the order: they are not to wear wreaths. Whoever has authority and does not do the righteousness of the Gospel is to be excluded and is not to pray with the bishop.

Whoever has received the authority to kill, or else a soldier, they are not to kill in any case, even if they receive the order to kill. . . .

A Christian is not to become a soldier. A Christian must not become a soldier, unless he is compelled by a chief bearing the sword. He is not to burden himself with the sin of blood. But if he has shed blood, he is not to partake of the mysteries [the sacraments], unless he is purified by a punishment, tears, and wailing. . . .[6]

Even after imperial persecution of the church ended, converts to Christianity serving in the army were aware that killing could not be regarded as a Christian action. There is, for example, the case of Saint Martin of Tours, both a military officer and a catechumen

---

4. Thomas Merton, trans., *Clement of Alexandria: Selections from the Protreptikos* (New York: New Directions, 1962), 27.

5. The oldest surviving manuscript was written not later than AD 340.

6. Hippolytus, *Canons* XIII-XIV.

preparing for baptism at the time. Refusing to take part in an impending battle, he said to Julian Caesar (better known to history as Julian the Apostate), "Hitherto I have served you as a soldier; let me now serve Christ. . . . I am a soldier of Christ and it is not lawful for me to fight." After offering to stand unarmed against the enemy, he was briefly imprisoned but then granted a discharge by Julian. Saint Martin went on to become a renowned bishop and theologian.[7]

St. Martin of Tours, cutting his cloak to share with a beggar

But since the Edict of Milan in AD 313, when the emperor Constantine became the protector rather than the enemy of the church, a collaborative relationship between state and church slowly began to develop which eventually meant Christians were as likely as pagans had once been to serve the emperor and, apart from those ordained as priests, to take up the weapons of war and kill in battle.[8] Though Constantine himself was baptized only on his deathbed and was thus an actual member of the church only in the final hours of his life, he nonetheless was a person whose life, at its best moments, was clearly influenced by the gospel. Yet not all his legacy, so far as the church is concerned, was positive. As Saint Jerome observed, "When the church came to the princes of the world, she grew in power and wealth but diminished in virtue."

The refusal to take up arms against enemies has always been remarkable, even scandalous, from the point of view of those in

---

7. *Butler's Lives of the Saints,* ed. and rev. Herbert Thurston and Donald Attwater (New York: P. J. Kenedy & Sons, 1963), vol. 4, pp. 310-13.

8. Church canons still bar anyone who has killed another human being from serving at the altar.

government as well as many others, who see no practical alternative to armed defense and the use of ever more powerful weapons. Even in the past hundred years, conscientious objection to participation in war has cost many men years of imprisonment and suffering, as well as execution in some cases. Since the founding of the church, thousands have given their lives rather than perform military service, among them people solemnly recognized as saints. Today every church upholds the right of conscientious objection, and many countries provide for the possibility of doing nonmilitary alternative service.

Note that conscientious objection to participation in war does not imply the rejection of using nonlethal force for self-defense or for the defense of others. It is only the rejection of deadly force. Let me illustrate the point with a story told by Metropolitan Anthony of Sourozh, who for many years led the Russian Orthodox Church in Great Britain. He recalled an encounter he once had during a retreat for university students. "After my first address one of them asked me for permission to leave because I was not a pacifist." "Are you one?" Metropolitan Anthony responded. "Yes," said the young man. "What would you do," Metropolitan Anthony asked, "if you came into a room and found a man about to rape your girlfriend?" "I would try to get him to desist from his intention!" the man replied. "And if he proceeded, before your own eyes, to rape her?" "I would pray to God to prevent it." "And if God did not intervene, and the man raped your girlfriend, what would you do?" "I would ask God who has brought light out of darkness to bring good out of evil." Metropolitan Anthony responded: "If I was your girlfriend I would look for another boyfriend."

Christian life, however peaceful, does not necessarily result in a tranquil life. Another passage in Matthew's Gospel rejects the idea that the life of Jesus' followers will be without conflict and division, even within families:

> *Do not think that I have come to bring peace on earth; I have come not to bring peace, but a sword. For I have come to set a man against his father and a daughter against her mother and a daughter-in-*

law against her mother-in-law; and a man's foes will be those of his own household. (Matthew 10:34-36)

The "sword" referred to here is not a deadly weapon but a symbol of the fractures that often occur within families and between friends when one chooses to live a life shaped by the Gospel. Jesus is not advocating division, only saying that the way of life he proposes will at times be a cause of discord that may even cut into the closest relationships. Living in a way that does not conform to dominant social patterns may lead to rejection and condemnation by those you dearly love. One has to take the risk, while doing everything possible to communicate love and respect for those who do not agree or cannot understand, at least not yet. Many Christians who refused to do military service have been disowned by one or both parents. More often, family life and friendships hold together but are made more brittle.

Consider, for example, the case of Franz Jägerstätter, one of the conscientious objectors to emerge within Hitler's Third Reich. He was fortunate that his marriage bore the weight of the stand his conscience led him to take, but his stand led to condemnation and rejection by many others, including both friends and relatives.

His is a life worth pondering. An Austrian farmer living in a hamlet, Saint Radegund, too small to warrant its own post office, Franz seemed, from a distance, a most ordinary man living an ordinary life. He held no academic degrees, was married and the father of three children.

He had not got off to a pious start in life. As a youth he was a local gang leader and had once been fined for being involved in a battle with a gang from a neighboring village. He had been the proud owner of a motorcycle. It is said that he fathered an out-of-wedlock child—and, in fact, was born out of wedlock himself. Nonetheless, his spirit was such that neighbors still regarded him as a *liaba mensch*—a "wonderful guy"—though a minimalist in his religious life.

In Franz's early twenties, there were signs that a change of heart and mind was occurring. He enrolled in voluntary religious classes conducted by the pastor of the Catholic parish in Saint Radegund.

His friends and neighbors must have been astonished. Perhaps it was less surprising that he was willing to raise embarrassing questions, asking, for example, if biblical texts did not suggest that Mary had other children besides Jesus.

Then when Franz was twenty-nine he underwent a change described by those close to him as "sudden and total." One neighbor commented, "It was almost as if he had been possessed by a higher power. It was so sudden that people just couldn't understand it." Franz began making regular pilgrimages to a nearby shrine and never passed a church without going in to pray. He was sometimes noticed interrupting his labor in the fields to pray. For a time he thought about joining a religious order, but ultimately decided in favor of family life. He and his wife, Franziska, chose to go on pilgrimage to Rome for their honeymoon.

With his religious awakening came a deepened social concern. In 1938, when the majority of Austrians voted in favor of national annexation with Nazi Germany, Franz (now thirty-one years old) resisted pressure from many neighbors and cast the village's only dissenting vote. Whenever anyone said "Heil Hitler," Franz responded, "To hell with Hitler!" His stand became the subject of fierce argument in the village tavern.

Blessed Franz Jägerstätter

That same summer Franz had a remarkable dream: "I saw a beautiful shining railroad train that circled around a mountain. Streams of children—and adults as well—rushed toward the train and could not be held back." What was the train's destination? In his dream Franz heard a voice say that the train was going to hell. Franz was as attentive to dreams as the two Josephs of the Bible. What was the shining train? It became clear to him that the train was Nazism. He realized that he and all the citizens of the Third Reich were among the passengers and that he had to make a choice between his religious faith and the demands of a political order that would make him one more passenger on Nazism's hell-bound train. Fidelity to his faith required resistance. "I would like to call out to everyone who is riding on this train," he wrote in his journal, "'Jump out of the train before it reaches its destination, even if it costs your life!'"

Like every able-bodied Austrian man, Franz Jägerstätter was called to do military service. His draft notice arrived in February 1943 when his oldest daughter was five. Ignoring the advice of his pastor, bishop, and many others, he refused to take the military oath, and for this he was immediately jailed.

Franz Jägerstätter was one of the least likely persons to question the justifications for war made by those in charge or to say no to the demands of his government. What did he know? He was only a farmer. He had never been to a university or a theological school. His formal education had occurred entirely in a one-room school-house. No priest, bishop, or theologian, no matter how critical some of them had been of Nazi doctrine, was announcing it was a sin to obey the commands of the Hitler regime when it came to war. So far as Franz knew, none of his fellow Catholics in Austria, even those who openly disagreed with Nazi ideology, had failed to report for military duty when the notice came. How dare so ordinary a person have such exceptional convictions?

His act of resistance moved those in positions of political author-ity in surprising ways. He was offered the possibility of noncomba-tant service, but after carefully searching his conscience, Franz said that it was not possible for him to wear the uniform, no matter what his own personal responsibilities might be. This sealed his fate. He was finally condemned to death and on August 9, 1943, was taken from his cell in Berlin's Brandenburg Prison and beheaded. Franz was thirty-seven years old.

His sacrifice was beyond measure: he loved his wife and children, his fields, his neighbors. Perhaps hardest of all was the knowledge that he was making decisions opposed by relatives and friends and contrary to the advice of his pastor and bishop. The bishop's views were unchanged even after the war. Years later, recalling his meeting with Franz, he wrote, "To no avail I set before [Jägerstätter] all the moral principles defining the responsibility carried by citizens and private individuals for the actions of civil authority. . . . Jägerstätter represents a completely exceptional case, one more to be marveled at than copied."

Franz's journal and letters from prison[9] make clear his conviction that not only the community of believers, the church, but the individual believer is called to bear witness, to prophesy and protest, even if he stands alone and is a person of modest social standing. Faith leads the believer to evaluate each choice in the light of eternity and faith. As Franz wrote from prison,

> *Just as the man who thinks only of this world does everything possible to make life here easier and better, so must we too, who believe in the Eternal Kingdom, risk everything in order to receive a great reward there. Just as those who believe in National Socialism tell themselves that their struggle is for survival, so must we, too, convince ourselves that the struggle is for the Eternal Kingdom. But with this difference: we need no rifles or pistols for our battle but, instead, spiritual weapons. . . . The surest mark of the follower of Jesus is found in deeds showing love of neighbor. To do to one's neighbor what one would desire for oneself is more than merely not doing to others what one would not want done to oneself. Let us love our enemies, bless those who curse us, pray for those who persecute us. For love will conquer and endure for eternity. And happy are they who live and die in God's love.*[10]

The Catholic prison chaplain in Berlin, who was often with Franz until his execution, said later: "I can say with certainty that this simple man is the only saint I have ever met in my lifetime."

---

9. See *Franz Jägerstätter: Letters and Writings from Prison,* ed. Edna Putz and with a biographical introduction by Jim Forest (Maryknoll, NY: Orbis Books, 2009).

10. Gordon Zahn, *In Solitary Witness* (New York: Holt, Rinehart & Winston, 1964).

"I have lost a dear husband and a good father to my children," his wife, Franziska, wrote soon after Franz's death, "but I can also assure you that our marriage was one of the happiest in our parish—many people envied us. But the good Lord intended otherwise, and has loosed that loving bond. I already look forward to meeting again in heaven, where no war can ever divide us again."

After the war Franz's ashes were brought to Saint Radegund and buried beneath a crucifix by the church wall. Little by little, his grave became a place of pilgrimage.

Through Archbishop Thomas Roberts, the retired bishop of Bombay, the Jägerstätter story made its way to the Second Vatican Council and helped the bishops endorse nonviolence and conscientious objection. In the 1960s, when Franz Jägerstätter's story became widely known through Gordon Zahn's book, *In Solitary Witness*, it helped encourage many draft-age American Christians to refuse military service in the Vietnam War. Now films and plays have been made about Franz Jägerstätter in both the United States and Germany. In December 1984, the president of Austria, responding to a national petition, issued a posthumous Award of Honor to Franz Jägerstätter. A postage stamp was issued bearing Jägerstätter's face. On the fiftieth anniversary of their honeymoon trip to Rome, Franz's widow returned to Rome, where she and the current bishop of Linz, Jägerstätter's diocese, were given an audience with Pope John Paul II. At the same time, the current bishop of Linz, with the support of Cardinal Koenig of Vienna, began a process that may lead to the official canonization of Franz Jägerstätter and has already resulted in his beatification.

Perhaps what would have astonished Franz more than anything else would have been to see, among the five thousand people packed into the Linz cathedral on the day of his beatification, that not only was Franziska, age ninety-four, present, but their children, grandchildren and great-grandchildren, sixty family members in all.

Times have changed. Yesterday's lonely dissenters, acting according to conscience and at times even ignoring the advice of church leaders, become today's saints.

Seeking Nonviolent Alternatives

"Deliver us from evil." As often as we say the Our Father, we make that appeal, most of the time without giving this short prayer much thought; but at times the words are said attentively and with desperate urgency.

There is a bitter ocean of evil in the world, expressed in a myriad of ways: lies, deception, cruelty, sexual abuse, rape, theft, bullying, enslavement, and so on. Evil happens in the smallest circles of life as well as the largest—within families and between nations. Often violence is involved, with injuries ranging from bruises and black eyes to grave or deadly injuries. In the case of war, countless people are killed and millions injured. In every kind of conflict, scars are left that are often invisible—post-traumatic stress disorder is widespread. Millions of people live from day to day on antidepressants and sleep medication, while others have become drug addicts. For many people hell is much easier to believe in than heaven. Hell is a familiar experience.

Getting free of the fragments of hell that have invaded one's life is a daily struggle. Yet Christian life is far more than the avoidance of evil. In the parable of a man from whom a demon was expelled, Jesus says,

> When the unclean spirit has gone out of a man, he passes through waterless places seeking rest, but he finds none. Then he says, "I will return to the house from which I came." And when he comes, he finds it empty, swept, and put in order. Then he goes and brings with him seven other spirits more evil than himself, and they enter and dwell there; and the last state of that man becomes worse than the first. (Matthew 12:43-45)

A strange parable. What's the point? One can turn to physics for an explanation. Vacuums are hungry and will draw in whatever is near at hand. Applied to the spiritual life, the point is that one may expel an evil spirit from one's life, but, unless something new and life-giving fills the vacated space, the vacuum that has been created may draw back not only the exiled evil spirit but seven others more malevolent than the first.

The parable suggests that a purely negative effort to get rid of self-destructive habits, however briefly effective, often creates an inner environment that eventually makes the situation even worse than it was. How many people do you know who have gone on a strict diet, shedding many pounds, but months later were heavier than ever before? Weight has been temporarily lost but the new habits needed to make weight loss permanent haven't been acquired.

It's much the same with violence. Passivity—refusing to answer violence with violence—is better than adopting the methods of one's adversary, but it's not enough. If we wish to be delivered from evil, surely part of the answer is to look for methods that work better than our flawed current solutions: nonviolent alternatives. In fact, that search has been going on for centuries and has not been fruitless.

The early Christian community astonished its hostile neighbors, low and high, by refusing to use violent means, whether in its own defense or under orders of its rulers. But the nonviolent witness Christians gave was only one aspect of a costly effort to convert their enemies, not destroy them. It is a good thing to do no harm but better to do good; good not to kill but better to save life.

This approach to conflict begins with a conscious aspiration to find solutions rooted in respect for life, including the lives of our enemies, and our hope that they too will benefit. While no one can be certain that he or she will always find a nonviolent response to every crisis that may arise, we can pray that God will help us find ways of resistance to evil that will not only avoid harming opponents but will involve better ways of solving problems that give rise to violence.

In the past century, partly thanks to movements associated with such leaders as Gandhi and Martin Luther King, that nonviolent struggle has become a widely recognized alternative to passivity on the one hand and violence on the other.

One could assemble a multivolume encyclopedia of stories from ancient times to our own that demonstrate the power of nonviolence to change both hearts and social structures. But in recent decades, as the technology of violence has made war more hellish than any evil it could be directed against, nonviolent approaches to conflict resolution have been increasingly taken up by those struggling for human rights and social justice.[1]

Because of my work with various groups that promote nonviolent approaches to conflict resolution, I've had the privilege of knowing many remarkable peacemakers, some quite famous but most of them known mainly in their own countries. I think, for example, of Mário Carvalho de Jesus, well known in Brazil but barely heard of in the rest of the world. Thanks to the work I was doing in the 1980s with the International Fellowship of Reconciliation, I got to know him. Mário is a Brazilian lawyer as well as a married man with seven children. A Christian religious awakening that he experienced while still a student in law school led him to a vocation committed to the poor. He went on to help found Servicio Paz y Justicia (Service for Peace and Justice), a network of Latin American social justice movements. He is also among the founders of the Frente National do Trabalho (the National Labor Front), a Brazilian workers' organization promoting the application of Christian social teaching through active nonviolence.

In the period 1964 to 1985, when a military junta ruled Brazil, Mário's involvement with the poor and with unions made him a target of the regime, with the consequence that he was repeatedly imprisoned. Remarkably, Mário has a gift for reaching out in a caring, disarming way to everyone, including enemies.

---

1. See the website of the Albert Einstein Institution for many examples of past nonviolent struggles and a catalog of nonviolent methods: http://www.aeinstein.org/.

During a strike, when police were sent to attack the workers, Mário led the strikers in chanting, "Long live the police!" He went up to speak to them, saying, "We are your brothers! Just as you have your uniform, we have our work clothes. If the law in Brazil were to protect rights, it would be we who would call you and ask you to come for our boss. But you needn't worry about us now that you're here. We will cause you no trouble. We will respect property and persons." Then he went on to tell the police why the workers were striking. The police decided not to break up the demonstration. Happily, forty-six days later, the workers won the agreement they were seeking.

During periods in prison, Mário was no less friendly to guards, nor was he resentful about being a captive. "Prison," he told me, "gives me the opportunity to pass the message of the gospel on to the police!"

"We must not be afraid to be imprisoned or to give our lives," he explained, "because it is fear that strengthens the political system. Remember the apostles when they were in prison and beaten. The apostles were beaten, but they were glad to give testimony to the truth of Christ. We have to prepare nonviolent activists to be pleased when they are imprisoned."[2]

Mário often explained active nonviolence to others:

> At first sight, the way of violence is the most impressive because it satisfies our aggressive impulses. But when you look at violence, you see that its promises never come true. At best, if you are lucky enough to be on the winning side, you find many of the people and places you wanted to protect are destroyed. You have a little space—this is called peace—before the next explosion. Violence also has the problem that it requires secrecy to be effective. You have clandestine meetings, and you have to distrust even the people you work with because there is always the chance that someone is a spy. Also, the factor of violence usually prevents the family from working

---

2. *IFOR Report*, a publication of the International Fellowship of Reconciliation, September 1981.

together for social change. It is self-sacrificing, which can be a good thing, but it has a tendency to corrupt and of its nature it destroys. Violence is always in a hurry. It thrives on fear, rage, hatred and aggression. It uses lies. Also we find no example of killing in the life of Jesus. Rather you see him speaking out against violence.

But active nonviolence does not seek the victory of one group over another but a change in which the whole society benefits. It is based on truth and love, not on domination. It is patient. It is willing to take time. It believes that, just as you and I have been converted so others, too, can be changed. Which of us is changed by threats? Rather than cause your enemy or innocent bystanders to suffer, the nonviolent person takes the suffering and does everything possible to protect the innocent. With active nonviolence, the whole family can take part, even the weak and old. We respect each person and believe each person has something good to do, something we all need. Nonviolence is not killing, but healing. As doctors try to heal broken bodies, we try to heal broken communities. And with nonviolence, we can always draw inspiration from the life of Jesus, who lives only by the truth and always gives us the example of healing.[3]

Yet another example is provided by the struggle in 1983 for democracy in the Philippines. How different the outcome would have been had it not been for the nonviolent commitment of so many people. In the final months before the dictator Ferdinand Marcos fled the country, "tent cities" for prayer and nonviolent training were set up in various centers of population. Returning from a visit with leaders of the nonviolent training movement in the Philippines, Hildegard Goss-Mayr wrote:

One tent was set in a little park right in the banking center in Manila, where the financial power of the Marcos regime was concentrated. Around the prayer tent, people who promised to fast and pray would, day and night, have a presence and carry within their fast and their prayer the whole revolutionary process. And I

---

3. From an unpublished interview with Mário Carvalho de Jesus by the author, Alkmaar, summer 1981.

think we cannot emphasize this enough: that in this whole process, there was always this unity of outward nonviolent action against the unjust regime and of that deep spirituality that gave people the strength later on to stand up against the tanks and to confront the tanks: this force of fasting and prayer. And in the celebrations of the Eucharist, they would point out that we are not fighting against flesh and blood, we are fighting against the demons of richness and exploitation and hatred that we have to cast out . . . from ourselves, from the military, from Marcos and his followers. . . . It makes a great difference . . . whether you promote hatred and revenge, or whether you help the people to stand firmly for justice but at the same time not to let themselves be taken in by hatred for those who stand with the oppressor. . . . [You learn] to stand for justice and to love your enemy . . . to the extent that you want to be liberated, you want to liberate him, you want to win him, you want to draw him in. You don't want his destruction but his liberation.[4]

It was precisely that spirit that led hundreds of thousands of unarmed people to fill the streets, block the tanks, and to reach out to the soldiers as brothers and sisters. "You are one of us," they said again and again. "You belong to the people." In the case of one detachment of soldiers sent to take control of a television station, with orders to shoot their way in if necessary, the people blocking the entrance greeted the soldiers and presented them with hamburgers and Cokes bought at a nearby McDonald's restaurant. The soldiers ate the hamburgers, drank their Cokes, and went back to their barracks.

On the 26th of February 1986, defeated by a nonviolent movement using what it called "people power," the reign of Ferdinand Marcos ended. He and his wife, Imelda, were flown by U.S. Air Force jet to Hawaii.

---

4. *Reconciliation International,* journal of the International Fellowship of Reconciliation, April 1986; also see "Nonviolence in the Philippines: The Precarious Road," *Commonweal,* June 20, 1986; and Jim and Nancy Forest, *Four Days in February* (Basingstoke: Marshall Pickering, 1988).

Holy Disobedience

THE LOVE OF ENEMIES often involves disobeying them rather than being their collaborators, a fact I am reminded of when I walk through the older parts of the small city I live in, Alkmaar, in North Holland. The current population is about 100,000, four times what it was during the Second World War. One special feature of Alkmaar is its centuries-old synagogue. Both Alkmaar and Amsterdam officially welcomed Jews at the time of their mass expulsion from Spain in 1492, but that aspect of Dutch life came to end in 1941 when Holland was occupied by the German Army. On March 5, 1942, 213 Alkmaar Jews—all the local Jews who were not in hiding—were gathered at the synagogue and from there transported, via Amsterdam and the Dutch concentration camp, Westerbork, to Auschwitz. Only a few survived; most were gassed and their bodies burned on the day of their arrival. The Alkmaar synagogue was closed.[1]

Auschwitz: one of the most hellish of words, two syllables that contain the names of all concentration camps, all places of annihilation. Here was constructed an immense factory for the assembly-line production of dead bodies, which were then converted into hair, gold fillings, and smoke. Auschwitz was a zone of absolute nihilism that made visible a demonic longing to murder God and to obliterate the divine image in humanity—a place for the death of conscience.

It had long been a hope of mine to go on pilgrimage to this Golgotha of the modern world. The chance finally came in November 2012, thanks to an invitation to give a lecture at a conference on interfaith dialog held at the University of Wroclaw in Poland.

I was one of three Orthodox Christians from outside Poland who came to the conference. The other two were Metropolitan Kallis-

---

1. In 2012 the Alkmaar synagogue was reopened.

tos Ware, longtime professor of Eastern Christian studies at Oxford, and Archimandrite Ignatios Stavropoulos, whose monastery is near Nefpaktos in Greece. With us were Father Vladimir Misijuk, a Polish priest and translator, and Dr. Pawel Wroblewski, one of the initiators of the conference in Wroclaw. The day after the conference ended, we traveled together to Auschwitz, now called the Auschwitz-Birkenau State Museum.

The local weather seemed to be in mourning—chilly, gray, on the edge of foggy. The area for miles and miles around Auschwitz is flat and thinly populated. The town near the camp, Oswiecim, is almost entirely of postwar construction—the prewar population had been removed by the Germans before construction of the concentration camp was started. This made sure that there would be no local witnesses.

Standing near Auschwitz's only surviving crematorium, our small group was met by a historian on the museum staff who led us into the camp's oldest zone, passing under the notorious *Arbeit Macht Frei* sign—Labor Brings Freedom.

I had imagined Auschwitz-Birkenau as one camp, but soon learned that Auschwitz served as the nucleus for more than forty other camps, with nearby Birkenau the point of delivery for the daily trainloads of captives, mainly Jews but also Christians, gypsies, homosexuals, and political opponents of the Nazis.

In Auschwitz itself, nearly all the buildings had been constructed of brick. It could pass for a solidly built military post. It would not have been hard to convince a naïve visitor, so long as he didn't look behind the wrong doors, that the conditions of life at Auschwitz weren't so bad. Why there was even an orchestra! On the other hand, were a visitor to be taken inside the buildings, he would have soon discovered that there are hells in this world worse than any hell he might imagine in the next. For example, there was Block 10—the domain of Nazi doctors carrying out the most vile medical experiments. One of the physicians, Josef Mengele, became known as the "Angel of Death."

Block 11 served as a "prison within the prison." A small court operated here at which many were sentenced to death. The basement cells were for those deprived of all food and water. Among those who died in one such cell, now marked by a tall paschal candle, was Maximilian Kolbe, a Franciscan priest who volunteered to take the place of a condemned fellow prisoner. Kolbe has since been canonized by the Catholic Church.

We stopped for a time in the yard between Blocks 10 and 11. This had been used as a place of summary execution for those convicted of breaking camp rules. Even a baseless accusation by an irritated guard could mean death before a firing squad. Here Metropolitan Kallistos led us in a prayer, long silences between each phrase, both for those who perished here and for the guards who, as prisoners of obedience, did most of the actual dirty work. We prayed with the awareness that, while the Nazis bear ultimate responsibility for what happened at Auschwitz, centuries of Christian anti-Semitism helped create an environment of contempt and hatred without which the Shoah would have been impossible. It is no comfort that the Nazis themselves despised Christianity and regarded its Jewish founder with contempt.

The charts, maps, photos, and exhibits we saw in the various buildings we passed through effectively told the story of the creation

Entrance to Auschwitz

and uses of Auschwitz and its surrounding network of camps: room after room containing the mute evidence of people who, after stripping naked for a delousing shower (so they were told), were gassed by the hundreds at a time—all children under fifteen, their mothers, the elderly, those judged unfit. Among those condemned on arrival, the lucky ones were those closest to the shower heads—they died immediately—while those farther away took up to twenty minutes to breathe their last. Among the exhibits were empty canisters of Zyklon B, the substance from which the lethal cyanide gas was released.

Our final stop in the original Auschwitz was the camp's one surviving place of gassing and body burning. It had escaped destruction because, when much larger gas chambers and crematoria were built at Birkenau, this smaller building had been converted into a bomb shelter. The adjacent crematorium, with its tall, square chimney and just two ovens, was also left intact.

Birkenau, about a mile away, didn't bother with brick structures for housing its captives. It was a vast gridiron of quickly erected wooden barracks filling a vast area, barrack after barrack as far as the eye could see. Though a small number of barracks survive, in most cases only the foundations remain. The single brick building left standing is at the entrance to Birkenau, a one-story structure crowned with an observation tower in the center under which prisoner-bearing freight trains arrived from every part of Europe. A few hundred yards beyond the station, truly the end of the line, was the area where an S.S. doctor presided over the selection process. Some were judged healthy enough to work—a slow death sentence for all but a few—while the rest were led away to the nearby gas chamber. About 75 percent were killed on arrival.

We visited two barracks, one of them still containing the deep wooden bunks on which inmates—up to a thousand per barrack—were stored at night like cigarettes in a carton. The shed-like structures provided almost no defense against the elements.

Walking from place to place in the two camps, I felt as if I had turned to wood. Words failed me—indeed my emotions failed me, and they still do. It's not possible to respond in word or sentiment in an adequate way to evil of such magnitude. The awful images are unerasable. Having been there in the flesh, the events that happened in this rural corner of Poland are forever engraved in me.

Any pilgrim to Auschwitz is brought closer not only to the people who suffered and died there but also to all the people who played roles, major and minor, in the Holocaust.

One thought kept running through my mind: this human-made hell could never have existed without obedience. Those who ran Auschwitz and all the similar camps, from the commandants to the lowest-ranking guard, decided that it was better to obey than disobey—better to be an executioner than a victim. While no doubt some of the personnel sent to Auschwitz were already psychopaths when they arrived, most of those assigned here were, at least at the start, ordinary people, no doubt relieved that they hadn't been sent into combat.

Adolf Eichmann, chief bureaucrat of the transportation system that delivered human cargo to the death camps, claimed at his trial that he had no ill feeling against Jews. He did what he did because it was his assigned duty. He was "just following orders." At his trial in Jerusalem he pointed out that he personally "never killed anyone." He was a good and loyal citizen, a patriot, doing only what his nation's law required of him.

The declaration that "I was just following orders" could be made not only by the staff of Nazi concentration camps but by all those who created and staffed the Gulag Archipelago or who dropped nuclear weapons on Hiroshima and Nagasaki or who firebombed Tokyo or Dresden or Coventry or London or who showered napalm and Agent Orange on Vietnam or, using drones, kill faceless human dots seen only on a computer screen. Obedience and duty are key words for all those today whose work involves killing or assisting those who kill. Only psychopaths want to kill. The rest of us who are caught up in one way or another in work that results in killing are, if not "just following orders," then being carried along by the political and economic currents of the society in which we happen to live. Better to go with the flow than dare to say no.

We would prefer people who do monstrous things to be monsters themselves. Unfortunately most of them are strikingly ordinary. As Auschwitz survivor Primo Levi wrote, "Monsters exist, but they are too few in number to be truly dangerous. More dangerous are the common men, the functionaries ready to believe and act without asking questions."[2]

I recall an Israeli friend, a child at the time of the trial, telling me how startled she was to notice, in a newspaper photo of Eichmann in his cell, that this enemy of the human race was wearing the same bedroom slippers that her father wore.

In his essay "A Devout Meditation in Memory of Adolf Eichmann," Thomas Merton reflected on the fact that the several psychiatrists testifying at Eichmann's trial found Eichmann normal, even perfectly sane. One of them said that Eichmann was "more normal, at any rate, than I am after having examined him."[3] Merton commented:

> *The whole concept of sanity in a society where spiritual values have lost their meaning is itself meaningless. A man can be "sane" in the limited sense that he is not impeded by disordered emotions from acting in a cool, orderly manner, according to the needs and dictates of the social situation in which he finds himself. He can be perfectly "adjusted." God knows, perhaps such people can be perfectly adjusted even in hell itself. And so I ask myself: what is the meaning of a concept of sanity that excludes love, considers it irrelevant, and destroys our capacity to love other human beings, to respond to their needs and their sufferings, to recognize them also as persons, to apprehend their pain as one's own?[4]*

Emily Dickinson expressed the same insight in just eight lines of poetry:

---

2. Primo Levi, *If This Is a Man* (Boston: Little, Brown, 1991), Afterword.

3. Hanna Arendt, *Eichmann in Jerusalem* (New York: Penguin Books, 1963), 25.

4. Thomas Merton, *Raids on the Unspeakable* (New York: New Directions, 1964), 45-49.

Much Madness is divinest Sense—
To a discerning Eye—
Much Sense—the starkest Madness—
'Tis the Majority
In this, as All, prevail—
Assent—and you are sane—
Demur—you're straightway dangerous—
And handled with a Chain—[5]

If a man like Eichmann is sane, we need to ask ourselves if sanity has come to mean merely the capacity to live successfully in society, no matter how toxic it is. In that case, God bless the mad. Clearly it's sane to regard having a successful career as more important than having an operating conscience. Sanity is to play it safe; sanctity is dangerous. God calls us to sanctity.

One of the ways the more ancient churches, Orthodox and Catholic, help us move toward sanctity is by identifying notable models of sanctity, canonizing them, and making sure they are remembered by putting their names on the church calendar. Thus, each day of the year provides an opportunity for us to discover and draw courage from one or more stories associated with a saint's life.

In contrast to Eichmann and the countless others who made themselves slaves of obedience, consider two recently canonized saints who, in the era when the crematorium chimneys of Auschwitz were flooding the sky with the smoke of genocide, were models of holy disobedience.

First consider Alexander Schmorell, canonized in 2012 at the Russian Orthodox cathedral in Munich,[6] the very city in which Hitler began his march to absolute power. Alexander Schmorell, a German medical student of Russian descent, was both a devout Orthodox Christian and also a co-founder of a small but significant anti-Nazi group that, at Schmorell's suggestion, christened itself the

---

5. *The Poems of Emily Dickinson: Variorum Edition* (Cambridge: Harvard University Press, 1998), poem 620.

6. An account of the canonization with many photos is posted at http://jimandnancyforest.com/2012/02/schmorell-canonization/.

White Rose. The group's name was inspired by the chapter "The Grand Inquisitor" in Dostoevsky's novel *The Brothers Karamazov*. In it we find ourselves in Seville during the height of the Inquisition. In this time of terror, Christ appears in the city's cathedral square, its pavement still warm from the burning of a hundred heretics the day before. Responding to a mother's desperate appeal, Christ raises from the dead a young girl, her daughter, whose open coffin is being carried across the square on its way to the cemetery. "The procession halts," Dostoevsky writes, "the coffin is laid on the steps at Christ's feet. He looks with compassion, and His lips softly pronounce the words, 'Maiden, arise!' and she arises. The little girl sits up in the coffin and looks round, smiling with wide-open wondering eyes, holding a bunch of white roses they had put in her hand." This merciful action completed, Christ is recognized by the Grand Inquisitor, who immediately orders his arrest.

In the context of the story, the white rose is a paschal symbol, a sign of the victory of life over death. The resurrection of the girl is set against the background of a world that seems to be under the rule of Satan, a world not unlike the Third Reich. The adoption of the name White Rose was the group's way of declaring their Christian conviction that he who has defeated death can also lift us from our graves—not only the grave to be dug at the end of our lives but the grave of fear-driven obedience that we occupy here and now.

Before their discovery and arrest, the members of the White Rose managed to publish and widely circulate a series of six open letters denouncing Nazi ideology and calling for resistance. One leaflet contained the only known public protest by any German resistance group specifically against the Holocaust: "Here we see [in the mass murder of Jews]," the text drafted by Schmorell declared, "the most frightful crime against human dignity, a crime that is unparalleled in the whole of history."

As was bound to happen, eventually the White Rose members were arrested, tried, and executed. Alexander Schmorell was beheaded on the 13th of July 1943. In his last letter to his family, he wrote, "This difficult 'misfortune' was necessary to put me on the right road, and therefore was no misfortune at all. . . . What did

I know until now about belief, about a true and deep belief, about the truth, the last and only truth, about God? Never forget God!" Thanks to a witness, we also have an account of his last words: "I'm convinced that my life has to end now, early as it seems, because I have fulfilled my life's mission. I wouldn't know what else I have to do on this earth."

Mother Maria Skobtsova (now Saint Maria of Paris) was a woman of similar courage living in the same period whose remarkable life began within the Russian Empire before the Bolshevik Revolution and ended in a German concentration camp. Along the way she was married twice, becoming the mother of three before she became a monastic. After her second marriage disintegrated, she was consecrated a nun by her bishop, Metropolitan Evlogy, who greatly valued the work she was doing among refugees.[7]

In 1933, twelve years before her death, she founded a house of hospitality and chapel on the Rue de Lourmel in Paris. One member of the core community that took root there was her son, Yuri. There was also a remarkable young priest, Father Dimitri Klépinin.

When Paris was occupied by the German army in 1940, it became a special priority of the community led by Mother Maria to assist the many Jews who came seeking shelter and help in escaping. Father Dimitri issued many false baptismal certificates. Under Gestapo interrogation, he was knocked to the floor after pointing out that Christ was himself a Jew. Remarkably, on that occasion he was released. The community and its allies smuggled many people—how many no one knows—out of Paris to the south of France or Switzerland.

In July 1942 came the mass arrest of 12,884 Jews. Almost 7,000 Jews, two-thirds of them children, were brought to a nearby sports stadium. Held there for five days, the captives were at last sent to Auschwitz. Mother Maria had often considered her black monastic robe and head scarf a godsend in her work. Now, with considerable bravado on her part, her habit opened the way for her to enter the

---

7. An excellent biography is available: Sergei Hackel, *Pearl of Great Price: The Life of Mother Maria Skobtsova, 1891-1945* (Crestwood, NY: St. Vladimir's Seminary Press, 1981).

Mother Maria Skobtsova

stadium. For several days she was able to work there, trying to comfort the children and their parents and distributing what food she could bring in. She even managed to rescue a number of children by enlisting the aid of garbage collectors, who smuggled the children out in trash cans.[8]

Early in 1943, the long-expected event happened: Mother Maria, Yuri, Father Dimitri, and another collaborator, Ilya Fondaminsky, were arrested. All four later died in concentration camps, in Mother Maria's case in Ravensbrück, not far from Berlin.

The last day of Mother Maria's life was Good Friday 1945. The shellfire of the approaching Russian army could be heard in the distance. Accounts vary as to what happened during the last hours of her life. According to one report, she was simply one of those selected to die that day. According to another, she took the place of a fellow prisoner, a Jewish woman.

Although perishing in the gas chamber, Mother Maria did not perish in the church's memory. Soon after the end of World War II, essays and books about her began appearing in French, English, and

---

8. The story is told in a well-illustrated children's book, *Silent as a Stone: Mother Maria and the Trash Can Rescue*, text by Jim Forest, illustrations by Dasha Pancheshkaya (New York: St. Vladimir's Seminary Press, 2007).

Russian. On the first day of May 2004, at Saint Alexander Nevsky Cathedral in Paris, Mother Maria, her son Yuri, Father Dimitri Klépinin, and their friend and co-worker Ilya Fondaminsky were officially recognized as saints.[9]

Perhaps the shortest expression of Mother Maria's credo is this brief sentence: "Each person is the very icon of God incarnate in the world." With this recognition, she said, comes the obligation to venerate the image of God in each person. She saw no other path to heaven except to participate in God's mercy. "The way to God lies through love of people," she explained. "At the Last Judgment I shall not be asked whether I was successful in my ascetic exercises, nor how many bows and prostrations I made. Instead I shall be asked, Did I feed the hungry, clothe the naked, and visit the sick and the prisoners? That is all I shall be asked."[10]

In Christian history, the holy disobedience these recent saints displayed is not at all unusual. The church calendar is packed with the names of saints who, in part due to their love of enemies, refused to follow orders, from the time of imperial Rome to our own day—men and women who refused to comply, refused to conform, refused to obey, refused to please the ruler, refused to reverence idols, refused to kill, refused to bear false witness, refused to renounce their faith, refused to ignore their suffering neighbor. Their holy disobedience to man was founded on the bedrock of their holy obedience to God. You find them on the church calendar on every day of the year. Many others are not yet formally canonized only because they have died too recently. There are martyrs dying today for their refusal to abandon their faith or adjust it to the demands of the society in which they live.

May Saint Alexander of Munich, Saint Maria of Paris, and all the saints who refused to please Caesar give each of us the courage to say no when a no is needed.

---

9. Among those participating in the event was Cardinal Jean-Marie Lustiger, archbishop of Paris, who subsequently placed St. Maria on the calendar of the Catholic Church in France.

10. A collection of her essays is available: *Mother Maria Skobtsova: Essential Writings* (Maryknoll, NY: Orbis Books, 2003).

A Life of Recognizing Jesus

DOROTHY DAY SO OFTEN repeated a saying of Saint John of the Cross that she made it her own: "Love is the measure by which we shall be judged." These few words summarize much of the gospel. The final weighing up of our lives, the Last Judgment, has to do with actively participating in God's mercy:

> When the Son of man comes in his glory, and all the angels with him, then he will sit on his glorious throne. Before him will be gathered all the nations, and he will separate them one from another as a shepherd separates the sheep from the goats, and he will place the sheep at his right hand, but the goats at the left. Then the King will say to those at his right hand, "Come, O blessed of my Father, inherit the kingdom prepared for you from the foundation of the world; for I was hungry and you gave me food, I was thirsty and you gave me drink, I was a stranger and you welcomed me, I was naked and you clothed me, I was sick and you visited me, I was in prison and you came to me." Then the righteous will answer him, "Lord, when did we see you hungry and feed you, or thirsty and give you drink? And when did we see you a stranger and welcome you, or naked and clothe you? And when did we see you sick or in prison and visit you?" And the King will answer them, "Truly, I say to you, as you did it to one of the least of these my brethren, you did it to me." Then he will say to those at his left hand, "Depart from me, you cursed, into the eternal fire prepared for the devil and his angels; for I was hungry and you gave me no food, I was thirsty and you gave me no drink, I was a stranger and you did not welcome me, naked and you did not clothe me, sick and in prison and you did not visit me." Then they also will answer, "Lord, when did we see you hungry or thirsty or a stranger or naked or sick or in prison,

163

and did not minister to you?" Then he will answer them, "Truly, I say to you, as you did it not to one of the least of these, you did it not to me." And they will go away into eternal punishment, but the righteous into eternal life. What you did to the least person, you did to me. (Matthew 25:31-45)

Is there any text in the four Gospels that involves more repetition of key words and phrases? It is a teacher's method of making sure his students get a crucial point: that Jesus identifies himself with those who are in urgent need and that the response we make to them is made to him. Those who seek mercy must practice mercy.

In almost any ancient church in Europe, one finds a visual representation of the Last Judgment: Christ occupying a throne, Mary his mother on one side, John the Baptist on the other, while below them, on one side, the blessed are processing into heaven while, on the other, the damned are being marched by grotesque devils into the jaws of a monstrous dragon.

At the Cathedral of Saint Lazarus at Autun in France, a church of exceptional beauty, an image of the Last Judgment is shown in relief on a huge half circle of stone resting over the great doors on the west porch. One of the finest Romanesque stone carvings ever made, the tympanum stops nearly all visitors in their tracks. In medieval times, the stone was brightly painted. The effect must have been even more stunning—and no doubt more alarming, a vivid reminder that the story we tell day by day and choice by choice with our own lives isn't guaranteed to have a happy ending. Though its central message is about hospitality, mercy, and salvation, the Last Judgment narrative includes a solemn warning: if we make hellish choices and lead a hellish life, we will land in hell. In fact, if we lead a hell-centered life, we're already there.

Autun's Last Judgment tympanum visually dramatizes the difference between those entering heaven and those going to hell. At its base, beneath Christ's feet and stretching the full width of the church's main entrance, is a long row of men and women standing on their coffins having been raised from the dead. A sword-bearing angel at the center of the figures looks with sorrow toward the wretched figures on the right whose lives have brought them damnation. As you gaze at these forlorn men and women, you notice that each of the damned seems trapped in himself. Not one of them notices another and none notices Christ. They didn't see him in life and don't see him in the afterlife either. In contrast, all the saved are gazing upward in enraptured amazement toward Christ.

The tympanum is one of the rare works to bear the artist's name: Giselbertus. Reading the Gospel according to Giselbertus, we learn that we are in heaven whenever we see Christ or are aware of his presence. Heaven is participation in God's being. It is seeing what has always been close at hand, what was always at the heart of reality, but somehow was barely recognized, glimpsed "as through a glass darkly" (1 Corinthians 13:12).

The imagery declares that, if I cannot find the face of Jesus in the face of those whom I regard as enemies, if I cannot find him in the unbeautiful and damaged, if I cannot find him in those who have the "wrong ideas," if I cannot find him in the poor and the defeated and damaged, then how will I find him in bread and wine or in the life after death? If I do not reach out in this world to those with whom he has identified himself, why do I imagine that I will want to be with him, and them, in heaven? Why would I want to be for all eternity in the company of those I avoided every day of my life?

On visits to the church at Autun and similar churches in other places, I have sometimes heard those gazing at images of the Last Judgment ask the question, "Why are we judged together and not one by one when we die?" The answer that makes the most sense to me is that history must reach its last page before God can fully weigh up the pluses and minuses of anyone's life. Our acts of love and failures to love continue to cast ripples until the end of time. What Adam and Eve did, what Moses did, what Herod did, what Pilate did, what the Apostles did, what Caesar Augustus did, what Hitler did, what Martin Luther King did, what Dorothy Day did, what you and I have done and left undone continue to matter and have consequences, for the better or the worse, for the rest of time.

It weighs heavily on many people that Jesus preached not only heaven but also hell. There are numerous references to hell in the Gospels, from the Sermon on the Mount onward. Many ask the question: how can a loving God allow hell to exist?

The only response to that question that makes sense to me was in a sermon I heard in an old gothic church in Prague in 1964 during my first visit to Europe. The preacher was a courageous man who, protesting Communist rule, had seen a great deal of prison from the inside. It is now too many years ago for me to repeat accurately what he said, but this is what I remember of it, or perhaps what it has come to mean for me.

God allows us to go wherever we are going. We are not forced to love. We are not herded into heaven. We are not coerced into recognizing God's presence. It is all an invitation. Hour by hour we make choices, some choices shaped by compassion and love, other choices shaped by fear, jealousy, anger, hatred, and pride. From childhood until we breathe our last, we choose. I hope, in God's mercy, that we can even make the choice of heaven in hell. But very likely we will make the same kinds of choices after death that we made so often before death.

In *The Great Divorce*, perhaps my favorite book by C. S. Lewis, there is a tour bus that leaves daily from hell taking its sullen passengers on an excursion to heaven. The bus, never full, tends to return with as many passengers as it started with, though anyone who wishes is free to make heaven their final destination. But the tourists from hell tend to find even the edge of heaven too bright and the blades of grass too sharp. It's all too fiercely real. Worst of all, they discover people in heaven whom they want to avoid at all costs.

The older we are, the more we replicate old choices and defend those choices, and make ideologies, philosophies, even theologies out of our choices. We canonize our choices by repetition. We can say not just once, as did Peter in the grip of fear, but day after day forever, "I do not know the man" (Matthew 26:72). We can say of all sorts of people we wish were elsewhere or dead: "He is worthless. He has no one to blame for his troubles but himself. His problems are not my business. He is an enemy. He deserves to die."

God's intention is that we should live. Isaiah described this in a vision of peace between creatures that seem born to enmity:

> *The wolf will live with the lamb,*
> *the leopard will lie down with the goat,*
> *the calf and the lion and the yearling together;*
> *and a little child will lead them.*
> *The cow will feed with the bear,*
> *their young will lie down together,*
> *and the lion will eat straw like the ox.*
> *The infant will play near the cobra's den,*
> *and the young child will put its hand into the viper's nest.*
> *They will neither harm nor destroy*
> *on all my holy mountain,*
> *for the earth will be filled with the knowledge of the Lord*
> *as the waters cover the sea.* (Isaiah 11:6-9)

The first issue of the *Catholic Worker* that Dorothy Day entrusted me with preparing for publication had an engraving by Fritz Eichenberg of the Peaceable Kingdom on its front page. Under the protective limbs of a great tree were a wolf and a lamb, a leopard and a goat, a rabbit and a bear, and in the center a child and a lion. All were safely at home with one another. It was a representation of paradise regained, the serpent no longer a dangerous tenant of the tree of life but resting harmlessly by the child's feet. This image of a life without enmity or bloodshed, the Peaceable Kingdom, is a revelation of the Kingdom of God.

We approach the Peaceable Kingdom by the everyday choices we make. At the heart of what Jesus displays in every action and describes in each parable is this: Now, this minute, we can be within the borders of the Peaceable Kingdom no matter in what circumstances we find ourselves. The way into it is simply to live in awareness of God's presence, a presence that includes those around us, even our enemies. Doing that, we learn the truth of what Saint Catherine of Siena said: "All the way to heaven is heaven, because Jesus said, 'I am the way'"—and one could add, "All the way to hell is hell."

There must be church people who, if only to themselves, occasionally admit to disappointment over Jesus' parable of the Last Judgment. Could he not have said something about the advantages of having been baptized and belonging to the right church and reciting the right creed? Would this not have been the right place for Jesus to say, "If you want to inherit eternal life, confess me as Lord and Savior and be saved"? Couldn't he have said that the Last Judgment would be a theological test and those who get the right answers will get the ultimate high grades? But it seems that Jesus, while using institutions, is not an institutionalist. His priority is mercy. Thus, the church he founded is called to bring us into the stream of divine mercy—not only that we should ourselves be beneficiaries of God's mercy but that we might become channels of mercy.

In the Liturgy of Saint John Chrysostom, immediately before the consecration of the bread and wine, there is the haunting phrase, "[Christ] gave himself up for the life of the world." This echoes a sentence in John's Gospel: "The thief comes only to steal and kill and destroy; I have come that they may have life, and have it to the full" (John 10:10).

Churches, as institutions, have sometimes failed dramatically in their vocation of mercy and safeguarding life. This has led many people to ask: "Does the church matter? Is it needed?"

My own answer is yes, we need the church. I hate to think where I would be without it—the times in my life when I have attempted to be a churchless Christian did not go well. We need the church but at the same time have to be on guard about its tendency, as an institution rather than a mystical reality, to make an idol of itself. We also need to be on guard about the tendency of religious leaders—in fact our own tendency—to forget, ignore, explain away, or bury in footnotes the more difficult parts of the gospel or to adjust it to fit within national interests and particular political outlooks or to disguise clerical careerism with a mask of piety. As the Orthodox pastor and theologian Father Alexander Schmemann noted, "There is nothing worse than professional religiosity."[1] Elsewhere in his journals he remarked, "The Church is most hindered by the Church itself."[2]

While church membership by itself will not save us, still we need the church. We need the church because Jesus has said that he is with us whenever two or three gather together in his name. We need the church for the Creed and for its guardianship of sacred texts. We need the church because we need to be part of a community of praise, of remembrance, of gratitude and reflection, of sacramental encounter. We need the church because Jesus called us to recognize him in the communal act of breaking bread. We need the church in order to be part of a community consciously seeking to be more aware that we are in God's presence no matter where we happen to be. We need the church to help us see beyond, and reach beyond, national borders, for Christianity has no borders and waves no flags. We need the church because we need a community that will help us learn to connect with people we might otherwise reject and condemn as enemies. We need a community of faith to help us experience God's forgiveness when, like those who failed to stop and aid the wounded man on the road to Jericho, we find ourselves living blind, indifferent lives, no longer aware that Jesus is hidden in those whom we avoid and in those we are ready to destroy. We need the church as a school of love, mercy, and healing.

---

1. *The Journals of Alexander Schmemann* (Crestwood, NY: St. Vladimir's Seminary Press, 2000), 32.

2. Ibid., 167.

Epilogue: Two Old People and a Young Man with a Gun

LET ME FINISH this book with a story that I've told before and will probably tell again. It has to do with an elderly couple and a young man with a gun. It's a story of protecting the life of an enemy by treating him as a welcome guest and, in the process, perhaps saving several lives, including their own. It's a story that demonstrates the truth of an insight of Saint John of the Cross: "Where there is no love, put love, and you will find love."

Louise and Nathan Degrafinried, both in their seventies at the time, lived in Mason, Tennessee. They were members of the Mount Sinai Primitive Baptist Church.

One morning in February 1984, Riley Arzeneaux, a man who escaped from the state prison several days earlier, came into their house. He aimed a shotgun at Louise and Nathan and shouted, "Don't make me kill you!"

Louise responded to this nightmarish event as calmly as a grandmother normally responds to the crises and accidents that befall a grandchild. "Young man," she said, "I am a Christian lady. I don't believe in violence. Put down that gun and you sit down. I don't allow no violence here." Riley obediently put the weapon on the couch. He said, "Lady, I'm hungry. I haven't eaten in three days."

While Nathan got their unexpected guest a pair of dry socks, Louise made a substantial breakfast: bacon and eggs, toast, milk, and coffee. She put out their best napkins.

When the three of them sat down to eat, she took Riley's hand in her own and said, "Young man, let's give thanks that you came here and that you are safe." She said a prayer and asked him if there was anything he would like to say to the Lord. He couldn't think of anything so she suggested, "Just say, 'Jesus wept.'" (A journalist later asked how she happened to choose that text. Louise replied, "Because I figured that he didn't have no church background, so I wanted to start him off simple; something short, you know.")

After breakfast she held Riley's hand again. He was trembling all over. "Young man, I love you and God loves you. God loves all of us, every one of us, especially you. Jesus died for you because he loves you so much."

Then the police arrived. Hearing the approaching sirens, Riley said, "They gonna kill me when they get here." But Louise said she was going out to talk to them. Standing on her porch, she spoke to the police in the same terms she had spoken to the convict: "Y'all put those guns away. I don't allow no violence here."

The police, as docile in their response to Louise as Riley had been, put their guns back in their holsters. Soon afterward, Riley was taken back to the prison. No one was harmed.[1]

Louise and Nathan Degrafinried might also have been killed, of course. Good, decent people die tragically every day. But actually it isn't so surprising that their warm welcome to a frightened man provided them with more security than any gun.

The story does not end with Riley's return to prison. Louise and Nathan were asked to press charges against him for holding them hostage but declined to do so. "That boy did us no harm," Louise insisted. As both she and Nathan refused to testify, the charges were dropped, though his prison sentence was extended for having escaped. Louise initiated correspondence with Riley. She asked for his photo and put it in her family album. Throughout his remaining years in prison—Riley was freed in 1995—Louise kept in touch with Riley and he with her. Louise actively worked for Riley's release. "He usually called on her birthday and around Christmastime," Louise's daughter, Ida Marshall, related to a reporter after her mother's death in 1998.

---

1. William H. Willimon, "Bless You, Mrs. Degrafinried," *Christian Century*, March 14, 1984.

Louise and Nathan Degrafinried

Louise had an enormous impact on Riley's life. "After looking back over all my life in solitary, I realized I'd been throwing my life away," he said in a 1991 interview. Riley recalls praying with Louise Degrafinried when she came to visit him in prison. "She started off her prayer," he recalled, "by saying, 'God, this is your child. You know me, and I know you.'" "That's the kind of relationship I want to have with God," Riley said. In 1988, Riley became a Christian. "I realized," he explained, "that meeting the Degrafinrieds and other things that happened in my life just couldn't be coincidences. After all that, I realized someone was looking over me."

Louise Degrafinried was often asked about the day she was held hostage. "Weren't you terrified?" a reporter wondered. "I wasn't alone," she responded. "My Savior was with me, and I was not afraid."

It's similar to a comment Riley made when explaining the events that led to his conversion. "Mrs. Degrafinried was real Christianity," he told mourners at her funeral. "No fear." Riley sat with immediate family in the front pew at the service and was among those carrying Louise Degrafinried's coffin to its burial place.

Louise and Nathan have died, but the story of their welcoming an escaped convict has become a parable of hospitality and the works of mercy: "I was on the run and you took me in, I was hungry and you made me breakfast, I was thirsty and you gave me coffee, I had wet socks on my feet and you gave me dry ones, I was ready to kill and you freed me from my weapon."

Acknowledgments

My gratitude goes first of all to Robert Ellsberg, publisher of Orbis Books and dear friend of many years, without whom this book would not have seen the light of day. I thank Yehezkel Landau, who years ago suggested I take a three-month sabbatical teaching and studying at the Ecumenical Institute for Theological Research, Tantur, on the road that links Jerusalem and Bethlehem; this text has its oldest root in my Tantur inaugural lecture given in the spring of 1985. I thank those who found time to read the book in manuscript and helped in many ways to improve the text: Tom Cornell, Harry Isbell, Shawn Storer, Monica Klepac, Michael Baxter, Brad Jersak, Addison Hart, Gerry Twomey, Pieter Dyckhorst, and Alex Patico. Finally, I bow to my wife, Nancy, a fountain of helpful advice and good cheer during the days and nights when these pages were being written.

December 10, 2013
Alkmaar, The Netherlands

Doing Good to Our Enemies: From a Fellowship of Reconciliation campaign, urging the White House to send food aid to China